PRAISE FOR *ART* *INTELLIGENCE FOR HR*

'By now you've heard plenty of talk about how artificial intelligence is the "next big thing" in technology and organizations and people need to be prepared for waves of new AI-powered tools, but what you have not heard is just how AI can and will impact the real work of HR and talent acquisition. Ben Eubanks' work fills that gap between awareness and understanding and provides real and practical ideas that can be utilized to drive success through AI technologies in your organization.'
Steve Boese, Conference Chair for the HR Technology Conference and Host of the HR Happy Hour Podcast

'So much has been said about the future of work, but the one thing we do know is that it will be affected by all kinds of automation, including artificial intelligence. HR professionals will need to understand how their own roles are changing while helping employees develop and prioritize the skills they will need for the age of disruption, and Ben Eubanks' take on how we can combine humans and technology paints a bright picture for the future of the HR profession.'
Mary Kaylor, Manager of Public Affairs, Society for Human Resource Management

'As we continue to recast and transform the new employment landscape in this millennium, Ben Eubanks' important work in HR research remains a vital key in producing collaborative results that not only promotes the profession of human resources, but also orchestrates tangible ROI benefits for employers. In this must-read book, he presents the contemporary and very real challenges of artificial intelligence that will change not only how we look at the world of work, but also how we approach what we do in the workplace every day.'
Dr Kim LaFevor, Dean of College of Business, Athens State University

'Already rapidly seeping into the workplace, artificial intelligence is giving savvy HR professionals and the communities they serve more data and more time to deliver better solutions and programmes. Ben Eubanks' thought-provoking book is a must-read for any organization committed to remaining competitive in the new and exciting frontier created by AI.'
Jeanne Achille, Program Chair, Women in HR Tech Summit, US and Asia, and tech entrepreneur

'In my many years leading HR and recruiting practices for various companies, I have always kept tabs on the technologies that have the opportunity to fundamentally change the landscape of what we do every day. Artificial intelligence has that capability, and Ben Eubanks' comprehensive coverage gives a deep look at how AI, automation and machine learning can revolutionize the way we hire and manage employees today.'
Kris Dunn, Chief Human Resource Officer, Kinetix

'As a learning and development professional focused on evaluating employee performance, I am keenly interested in ways where we can leverage intelligence and data to answer questions and inform decisions. Artificial intelligence, as outlined in Ben Eubanks' book, is one of the key ways I see businesses becoming more agile and competitive in the digital age through a mix of automation, augmentation and personalization.'
Kevin M Yates, Fact-Finder for Learning and Development, McDonald's

'As always, Ben Eubanks takes a topic as complex as artificial intelligence and presents it in a way that is understandable for people at all levels of technical proficiency. *Artificial Intelligence for HR* is a must-read for any business leader concerned with the impact this emerging technology has, and will have, on the modern workforce.'
George LaRocque, Founder and Principal Analyst, HRWins

'As a technology leader within the learning industry, I often have to remind business leaders that technology is just a component of the overall puzzle. In the end, people are a critical part of the business, and Ben Eubanks' book focuses on how we can blend the best that people bring to the table with the best that machines and algorithms have to offer in an exciting way.'
Skip Marshall, Chief Technology Officer, Tribridge

'Ben Eubanks has written a must-read book for all human resource professionals. His insight and knowledge around the challenges of this ever-changing world of technology and artificial intelligence in human resources is one of the best in the industry!'
Kristi Jones, Manager, Talent Acquisition, H&R Block

'I've seen hundreds of presentations on HR topics in my role, and I know that topics often get overhyped in the short term and under-deliver in the long term. Artificial intelligence is the next frontier for HR to conquer, and Ben Eubanks' book is the first step down that path for HR executives.'
Shane York, Vice President of Events, Human Capital Institute

'For the last 30 years people have worried about computers and machines taking work away from humans. In reality, these tools have progressively offered greater opportunities for humans to discover and hone new skills thanks to this intelligent automation, and this book sheds light on how the human resources profession benefits from the latest AI-related technological advances.'
Riccardo Antonelli, International Division Coordinator, GEMA Business School (Rome, Italy)

'Change is inevitable, especially in the world of work. Ben captures both the advent of AI and its potential future in a way that shows how HR and business will evolve. His approach is spot on and makes the future of AI intriguing and not threatening.'
Steve Browne, SHRM-SCP, VP of Human Resources, LaRosa's, Inc

'As a global HR influencer, I am always looking for resources and insights that will help today's HR, talent and L&D leaders improve their capabilities. *Artificial Intelligence for HR* offers a compelling look at how today's cutting-edge technologies can play a role in improving the performance of HR teams for businesses around the world.'
Mostafa Azzam, Managing Director, The HR Talent

'Today's experience-driven employer relationship requires a keen focus on the individual. As Ben Eubanks' book demonstrates, AI technologies are going to help HR leaders personalize the employee experience and create more human relationships in powerful, scalable ways.'
China Gorman, Managing Director America, UNLEASH

'I have researched the HR and recruiting technology industry for many years, and one of the hottest trends I'm watching is how artificial intelligence will impact the employee experience. Ben Eubanks is a leading expert in this space. His book offers a great overview of the technology providers along with the use cases that deliver value to today's business leaders.'
Madeline Laurano, Co-Founder and Chief Research Officer, Aptitude Research Partners

Artificial Intelligence for HR

Use AI to support and develop
a successful workforce

Ben Eubanks

First published in Great Britain and the United States in 2019 by Kogan Page Limited

2nd Floor, 45 Gee Street	c/o Martin P Hill Consulting	4737/23 Ansari Road
London	122 W 27th St, 10th Floor	Daryaganj
EC1V 3RS	New York, NY 10001	New Delhi 110002
United Kingdom	USA	India

www.koganpage.com

ISBNs

Hardback   978 0 7494 8782 9
Paperback   978 0 7494 8381 4
eBook   978 0 7494 8382 1

British Library Cataloguing-in-Publication Data

A CIP record for this book is available from the British Library.

Library of Congress Cataloging-in-Publication Data

Names: Eubanks, Ben, author.
Title: Artificial intelligence for HR : use AI to support and develop a
   successful workforce / Ben Eubanks.
Description: 1 Edition. | London, N.Y. : Kogan Page Ltd, [2018] | Includes
   bibliographical references.
Identifiers: LCCN 2018039699 (print) | LCCN 2018041240 (ebook) | ISBN
   9780749483821 (ebook) | ISBN 9780749483814 (pbk.) | ISBN 9780749487829
   (hardback) | ISBN 9780749483821 (ebk)
Subjects: LCSH: Personnel management. | Labor supply. | Artificial
   intelligence.
Classification: LCC HF5549 (ebook) | LCC HF5549 .E828 2018 (print) | DDC
   658.300285/63–dc23
LC record available at https://lccn.loc.gov/2018039699

Typeset by Integra Software Services, Pondicherry
Print production managed by Jellyfish
Printed and bound by CPI Group (UK) Ltd, Croydon, CR0 4YY

*To my four Bs, be sure to chase your dreams
if you want to catch them.
Melanie, thanks always for your love and support.
You make me a better person.*

CONTENTS

ABOUT THE AUTHOR

Ben Eubanks is an author, speaker and researcher. He spends his days as the owner and Principal Analyst at Lighthouse Research & Advisory.

He has authored hundreds of reports, ebooks and other resources over the course of his career. He also maintains upstartHR, a blog that has touched the lives of more than 1 million business leaders since its inception. He is the host of We're Only Human, a podcast that examines the intersection of talent and technology in the workplace through interviews with business leaders, researchers and other insightful guests. We're Only Human is one of the featured shows on HR Happy Hour, the world's longest-running HR podcast network.

Previously an HR executive for an Inc. 500-ranked global technology startup, he currently operates Lighthouse Research & Advisory, a human capital research and advisory services firm. He works with HR, talent and learning leaders across the globe to solve their most pressing business challenges with a research-based perspective tempered by practical, hands-on experience. He also supports technology vendors with a wide variety of content, thought leadership and advisory services.

Most importantly, he has four children, a wonderful wife of 10-plus years and a preference for running in a variety of outlandish races for fun.

FOREWORD

Artificial Intelligence. The very words conjure up images of robots taking over the world. And, after all the science-fiction movies over the last forty to fifty years or so, of course it would. We've long been fascinated with the idea that a robot can be like a human; that a robot can perform human tasks. But, when you look back to the early years of robotics, the thought of a 'thing' having any type of artificial, human-like intelligence seemed like a dream for far into the future.

Today, those dreams are now a reality. Although still in its early stages, artificial intelligence as it relates to employees and the work we do is quickly becoming something that human resources leaders need to be aware of and educated about. This adds to the ongoing arsenal of tools and topics that HR is responsible for. Do you remember 10 years ago when this thing called 'social media' was new and something we all had to learn from a business perspective? It seemed very scary because of all the unknown factors. We quickly got up to speed, researched and wrote policies and procedures to prepare. Transparently, we also failed on some, rewrote them and reexamined our approaches. What we learned from that experience is HR professionals need to be keenly aware of how technological advances and communication impact the workplace. We also have to be at least a step or two ahead of the rest of the employees so that we provide the insight and advice our organizations need.

Artificial intelligence in the workplace is similar. We cannot turn a blind eye, or say, 'We will learn about this later.' Later is too late. The fact that you are reading this book means that you have taken the first of many positive steps in not only expanding your knowledge and opinions of AI and how to use it, but it also means that you are forward thinking in how it applies to your organization. What are the areas your employees are currently not working in an effective manner? How can technology be used to supplement the existing workflows in order to increase productivity or engagement?

As you dive into each chapter, there are a few things to keep in mind to help ensure you make the most of the journey. First, be open-minded. Since the capabilities of machine learning are constantly developing, so are our reactions and applications of that learning. Artificial intelligence and machine learning can be scary for many people. Coming back to the notion of robots taking over our jobs, employees may be under the impression that AI will help replace them. We know that HR is cast as the watchdog of our organizations in terms of keeping the status quo, maintaining continuity and minimizing risk. This is one time where that will not benefit your organization, your employees or your own development. Read each chapter with a curious, open mind. Really consider whether each suggestion or example could make you or your organization better, more productive or more engaged.

Next, think about the impact to process and workflow. Organizations tend to get stuck in their old ways and do not make time to reexamine them very often. Use this opportunity to think about the current processes you have in place and how artificial intelligence can positively impact changes and improvements in the workflows. The opportunity for you as an HR professional to positively impact these workflows is great. It opens you and your team up to circumstances that require strategic planning. In fact, you may find that before you adopt some of the technologies enhanced by artificial intelligence, you need to go through a needs assessment and make changes to existing processes and workflows. This is a common challenge with any technology selection and implementation. After all, who wants to automate the wrong processes?

Finally, think about change management. Artificial intelligence and how it will be applied can cause angst or concern for many people today. As you gain understanding, think about not only how AI will affect your organization from an operational standpoint, but how you'll begin to craft messages to explain the potential impacts. How will you get buy in from all levels of the organization? What will each stakeholder group appreciate and be concerned about regarding artificial intelligence? How can you and your team proactively address these concerns?

These are just a few ideas to get you started down the path of greater understanding with artificial intelligence. Now, what are you waiting for?

Trish McFarlane
CEO and Principal Analyst, H3HR Advisors

PREFACE

My career has led me places I never imagined going, but I wouldn't have had it any other way. When I was a child I wanted to work in human resources before I even knew what it was. Seriously. For a profession that so many people 'fall into', I chose HR as a career path on purpose. For starters, I was the older middle child. My three brothers depended on me to be the peacemaker and mediator for disputes, and because I didn't have any position of authority, I had to keenly hone my influence and negotiation skills. More practically, my parents have owned a small business since I was a child, and I always saw the troubles they had with hiring, motivating and retaining their people. As an entrepreneurially minded child I thought to myself, 'If I can just get a degree in business and find out how to solve this problem, I will forever be in demand.' Fast forward to college, and a professor asked me to write a paper on this thing I had never heard of called 'human resources'. Honestly it sounded incredibly boring, but once I started researching what it was, I realized that HR was exactly what I had always wanted to do with my life and my career. I graduated with my degree in human resources management and got to work.

I started my career as a lot of HR professionals do, dealing with stacks and stacks of employee files and all of the administrative fun that comes with that. Over time I worked my way through several positions until I was working as an HR executive at a fast-growing technology startup, and the challenges and pace of business kept me on my toes. I gathered my HR certifications along the way and still maintain them to this day, a tribute to my roots and a reminder that in spite of all the neat things technology can do, it will never replace the capability of great people. Throughout this period of time, I had been writing and blogging as a side hobby about my experiences working and learning in HR, and a friend reached out to see if I wanted to take on a role as an analyst in the HR industry. The way I remember her explaining it was, 'You already like writing and

speaking, but now this can be your job. Plus, you get to do research.'
I was sold. I moved into an analyst firm and soaked up everything I
could about the industry before moving on to run my own firm,
which is where I am today.

I have the most amazing job, if I'm going to be honest. Each day
presents opportunities to connect with leaders from across HR and
business, helping them achieve their goals. Additionally, I spend a
considerable amount of time learning from the vendors about their
technologies and how they operate, often advising them on product
strategy or market trends. The research I get to do every day excites
me, and it gets me closer to my own personal life's mission: making
HR better, one HR pro at a time. Every time I educate someone, including yourself, it is the proverbial rising tide that lifts all boats. We
all get better when one of us gets better.

However, this book isn't about my past or my biography. That's
short enough to fit into a few short paragraphs above, for the most
part. This book is about one of the research efforts I've undertaken
that I believe has the chance to fundamentally change the HR profession in ways that have never before been seen. Technology has always
been a part of how HR operates. While software is the focus of this
book and is also what we think of when we discuss technology, it's
important to remember that even paper is a technological improvement over raw memory. I believe we are on the cusp of an incredible
shift in the technology landscape that has the capability to affect how
HR gets done at companies around the world. Artificial intelligence
technologies are shaking up industries like healthcare, cybersecurity
and retail. However, those changes are also affecting specific functions in the business, such as marketing, customer services and business operations. There are tremendous amounts of resources out
there focusing on some of those other aspects of how artificial intelligence will change industries or functions, but when I started this
research project there was nothing clear cut about how this will affect the profession of HR that I know and love.

The field of HR really needs a special touch. It's not just enough to
understand the technology. Lots of people are technical in nature and
can't relate it back to the human impact on the workplace. The right

approach is to look at the problem from the other end of the spectrum: what challenges do businesses face when dealing with candidates, employees and non-employee talent, and how can technology help to resolve those? I'd like to think that my background as an HR executive helps to ground me and my research so that it takes on a very practical flavour. I'm not interested in hype. I've had to go to my CEO with people-related challenges and know that there is no margin for putting your faith in an unreliable or unrealistic technology. I'm also not an academic – any research effort I take on needs to have the potential to improve the lives of HR, talent and learning leaders by giving them better information or tools to improve their performance and results. Perhaps most importantly, my fundamental belief is that *artificial intelligence has the opportunity to make HR more human, not less*. I'll explore that notion at some level in virtually every chapter, saving the deep dive for the final chapter, where I talk about the skills you need for success in the era of artificial intelligence.

This book has been written with these concepts in mind. I've gone as far as possible to make it practical, insightful and helpful. I've provided examples and case studies everywhere I could to give you the insights you need to apply the concepts and principles the chapters explore, not just consume them and move on. And, as I've realized, the technological landscape is always changing. Some of the companies and functionalities I talk about in this book will change over time, and that's fine. It's a fact of life. That's the warning label you need when writing a book about a cutting-edge technology that is still evolving rapidly, but I did my best to clarify what technologies are available today and what technologies I envision becoming available in the future.

I know your time is valuable, so I want to close by thanking you for your time and attention in reading this book. Based on the feedback I've received from those that have heard me talk about the concepts within the following pages, it will be well worth your time. I'm writing about this topic because I'm passionate about it and passionate about improving the field of HR.

ACKNOWLEDGEMENTS

This book has been quite the undertaking and I have done my very best to ensure that I give appropriate credit to everyone within the context of each chapter who offered insight or ideas that supported the content. That said, there's always someone who is left out of the final product, so I'll just say this: if you and I have interacted, connected or collaborated over the course of my career, there's a good chance some measure of that influence made its way into this book. I am who I am because of the people I surround myself with, and I'd like to think that I surround myself with good kinds of people. To each of you, I say thanks!

Two of the special people I can't imagine being here without:

Trish, you've taught me more about collaboration than I could have ever learned on my own. I appreciate you.

Christine, your leadership and guidance helped me early in my career and prepared me for the path I've taken. You're still the best boss I ever had.

A snapshot
of HR today

In 2014, Carnegie Mellon had some of the world's brightest robotics minds working on its campus. These scientists were focused on the bleeding edge of robotics, improving upon the capabilities of existing technology and leveraging research to design new systems. Their insights, developed within a university setting, could have created new breakthroughs and advancements in the use of robotic technology for the betterment of mankind.

But then, virtually overnight, they all left.

In a surprise move, Uber had lured the scientists away, hiring a significant portion of Carnegie Mellon's robotics talent in a single sweeping move. This hiring spree was a step forward in the firm's strategic pursuit of a self-driving fleet of automobiles, but it clearly caught Carnegie Mellon by surprise. Looking back, it's hard to blame the educational institution for not seeing this upstart technology firm as a threat. Logically, when Carnegie Mellon considered its peers in the marketplace, it evaluated other top-shelf universities and research think tanks as competitive threats. However, it didn't consider the possibility of a ride-sharing service snagging its highly prized robotics talent.

What this means for today's business leaders is that it's no longer enough to simply look at the two or three long-term competitors to keep a finger on the pulse of the industry. New competition can come from any direction. And company leaders are funny in that they always think that they are somehow shielded from the impact of these new technologies and business models. It's a great example of what happens when firms only consider their traditional competitors and markets instead of broadening their perspective. This is a small example of disruption and how it impacts the workplace, but it signifies a larger change that leaders must take seriously in order to remain competitive.

This story offers a clear understanding of the concept of industry convergence, just one of the many trends shaking up the workplace today. In a recent global study of Chief Human Resources Officers (CHROs),[1] IBM found that the number one concern for these talent leaders was industry convergence. A good example of this comes from the competition between Carnegie Mellon and Uber,[2] but others exist as well. For example, in a discussion with a Canadian banking and financial services employer with tens of thousands of employees, one of the HR executives was quick to redirect the conversation when industry was mentioned. He claimed the firm was a technology company first and a financial services institution second. This convergence means that more employers are looking to hire technical engineering talent, even if they aren't in traditional technology industries, tightening the labour market for sought-after software engineers.

Look around you. Today's human resources practice is not the same as that of years past. More and more companies are looking for ways to leverage their people as a strategic differentiator, giving them an edge over the competition. New technologies and tools are shifting the conversation for HR and business leaders, enabling them to have greater insights into organizational functions, outcomes and variables. Yet in spite of all of this, there are challenges that we simply can't seem to shake. Globalization is forcing employers to change how they have traditionally approached markets and talent. Disruption is affecting businesses in a wide spectrum of ways, from changes in consumer preferences to radical departures from traditional business models and methods. And greater demands for delivering memorable, engaging employee experiences continue to stress out HR leaders that are doing more with less. New technologies like artificial intelligence seem to offer some glimpse of hope, but many human resources and business executives find themselves asking how these tools work and what they actually do. Are they marketing hype? Are they actual solutions to everyday problems? What can help businesses survive and thrive in a competitive market full of disruption?

The age of disruption

The age of disruption is a blend of multiple competing priorities. Not only does this idea of industry convergence factor into the puzzle, but the way employers acquire talent is shifting as well. Employers are moving away from the traditional 'buy and hold' approach to a more flexible, nimble version based on project work and a variety of non-traditional worker types. Yes, for as long as there have been workers there have been side gigs, which can include freelancing, contracting, or other short-term assignments. However, while the concept of 'gigs' isn't anything new, the platforms available today give workers more and more control over how their time can be exchanged for money. In economics terms, it reduces the *friction* of the labour market, making it easier to match up skills with those that want to pay for them. Fiverr allows designers and other workers to offer their skills in small projects with a range of compensation depending on their experience and quality. Taskrabbit allows users to hire someone for small tasks, such as a quick grocery store trip or coming into an office to file some paperwork. And the popular ride-sharing apps now give virtually any consumer the ability to push a button and have a vehicle appear within minutes to take them anywhere they want to go. From an employer perspective, applications like Wonolo and Shiftgig do the same thing – they essentially enable employers to push a button and have contract workers show up ready to work. While their workload is often around more labour-intensive or low-level tasks, it's a foreshadowing of the future when more and more work can be handled by non-employee talent. Plus, this whole gig segment of the workforce is increasing rapidly. Research from Princeton University shows that the platform gig economy grew tenfold between 2012 and 2016.[3] While this seems like a small piece of the overall economy, if these platform gig workers were aggregated together as a single employee population of 800,000 workers, the company would be larger than Target and General Electric combined.[4]

This doesn't even take into account the changes in data and technology. Today, firms collect data on virtually everything. Every interaction. Every connection. All of this information, aptly termed 'big data', is being gathered, yet employers still struggle to make sense of the information in ways that can add value to the organization. This is true even more so for employee-focused data, because while marketing and sales tools have been more insights-driven over time, HR and talent systems are just reaching this level of maturity. In the Lighthouse Research 2017 Business Value of HR Technology research study, my firm found a variety of interesting insights. For instance, business leaders working outside HR are twice as likely as HR leaders to see human resources technology as a *strategic* tool, not just an *administrative* one. Data takes a central position in the discussion in the following chapters due to its role in empowering the technologies that businesses leverage today.

On the worker side of the equation, employees also now have greater expectations of the technology they access and utilize in the workplace. Consumer technology preferences for intuitive software applications that are mobile friendly and available anytime, anywhere are now commonplace. This is intriguing because even as recently as five or ten years ago, the bulk of the workforce didn't have any real say-so in how companies adopted and leveraged HR technology. In fact, virtually all of the technology adopted was done so purely with the administrators in mind. The question asked when looking at technology solutions was, 'What makes it easier to do HR, learning, or recruiting work?' However, today employees often have access to self-service tools for a range of needs, from tracking competencies and performance to updating personal information. That means employees now have yet another lens through which to evaluate their employers. As we'll see in the coming chapters, some of those tools are powered by artificial intelligence technologies that can offload HR tasks and improve user satisfaction at the same time. And if it sounds like a relatively minor item, our research shows otherwise. This type of technology can actually influence the employee experience – our research shows that high-performing firms (see definition below) are *eight times less likely* to say their HR technology is troublesome, a simple but effective metric for evaluating software usability.[5] And many studies in recent years put usability at or near the top of the list of requirements when evaluating vendor options, which means it's no longer a 'nice to have' but a 'must have' for enterprise HR software buyers.

Defining 'high-performing'

One of our standard research practices is to attempt to separate out high-performing companies from the rest by asking employers in our surveys to explain changes in key performance indicators over time. Those KPIs are then used to signify if an employer is a 'high performer' or not. The specific metrics we use are revenue, employee retention and employee engagement, as they are linked in a large body of research to each area of the business.

For instance, revenue is related to business health, but it also signifies a positive customer experience because satisfied customers spend more, are more likely to purchase again, and are likely to refer other customers. Employee retention signifies a positive employee experience across a range of areas, and retention directly impacts company profitability. Engagement not only signifies a positive workplace experience, but other business areas as well. Several studies correlate engagement with profit, innovation, customer satisfaction and more. The three elements of revenue, retention and engagement paint a picture of organizational health and give us a valuable measure by which to cut our research data.

It is common to see drastic differences in employer practices based on whether the firm is a high performer or not by our standards. Consider these three examples:

1 In our Business Value of HR Technology study, the research shows high-performing firms are eight times less likely to say their HR technology is troublesome.

2 Our Performance Management, Engagement and Business Results study pointed out these talent practices that high performers were more likely to implement: frequent goal-setting, recognition for performance, in-the-moment feedback, developmental coaching and peer feedback. Low performers were more likely to prioritize annual reviews and trying to develop employee weaknesses.

3 Our latest Learning Content Strategy study showed that high-performing firms were more than twice as likely to be using a cohesive strategy to guide learning content development and delivery, and they were also twice as likely to be measuring learning impact and outcomes.

While this isn't the only way to measure success, it provides a powerful lens through which to analyse practices and approaches that high-performing companies have in common. Within the context of this book, any mentions of high-performing practices are based on these criteria.

Researching and understanding HR today

The research practice our team leads has uncovered a wide variety of insights in the last few years, and they paint a picture of HR that requires more sophisticated practitioners and tools than those of yesterday. Across the spectrum of human capital management, from talent acquisition and employee development to talent mobility and engagement, greater demands are being placed on the human resources function to deliver tangible, actionable business results. Some examples of shifting trends are included below to help set the stage for discussions to come around specific human capital management functional areas.

Talent acquisition

Today's hiring climate is a candidate's market, which was confirmed in a recent research interview with the founder of a talent acquisition technology firm. In the discussion, the founder explained that he is seeing incredible pressures not just in normally challenging fields like software engineering or nursing but in other areas as well, such as sales or skilled trades. His belief is that candidates have more power than ever to demand what they might want in a role, and those demands change how the company recruits and interacts with the candidate population. The reason he founded his firm is because the entire online job search process is disappointing and frustrating for candidates. His team's research shows that nearly three-quarters of people would agree that online job search is a frustrating process. This is driving a change in technology and company behaviours to deliver a better candidate experience.

Candidates also want more interaction in the application process – our research tells us that when candidates apply for a job, they want a chance to really show what they're made of. While it's often been thought that elements of the hiring process like assessments were disliked by applicants, the data actually says that they *like* those aspects but only if they actually make them more competitive for the job. In other words, we don't want a generic psychometric test, we'd much prefer a job simulation that allows us to showcase relevant skills and knowledge.

At the end of the day, candidates are looking for a more personalized experience, and yet recruiters and employers are struggling to keep pace with hiring needs on a global scale. The Lighthouse Research 2017 Talent Acquisition Priorities[6] study found that talent acquisition leaders were focused heavily on improving their relationship with the business and improving their practice, but the primary areas of hands-on recruiting that they wanted to fix were onboarding and sourcing. In virtually every research study on talent acquisition I've conducted or seen in the last few years, sourcing technical talent always rises to the top of the list. Another research project pointed out just how challenging it is to scale globally. While today's workplace is more globalized than ever before, employers still struggle with the leap to international operations. Seven out of ten employers with a global presence are not fully confident in their knowledge of foreign compliance requirements, and four in ten employers are spending more than four hours per month, per employee, to onboard, pay and manage global workers (Lighthouse Research, 2017).[7] This hampers not only HR's productivity, but the ability to influence and impact performance across the enterprise.

Talent mobility

Employees want to own not just their jobs, but their careers as well. The first research project I ever completed focused on entry-level HR professionals and their primary needs, and one of those turned out to be a very clear career path. Fast-forward 10 years, and the data I'm seeing now from other sources validates those findings in that employees and job applicants are hoping not just for a job, but for a longer-term career track that they can plan for. The intriguing intersection of this, however, is that employees are perceived as staying at jobs for less time than in years past. This perception continues to drive decisions, spending, and resource investment, despite the fact that it has no basis in reality. The United States Bureau of Labor Statistics reported in 1983[8] that the average workplace tenure was 4.4 years. If we believe the current narrative, the current records should show a sharp decline in this tenure number because of job hopping and unrest in the employee population. Yet data from 2016[9] shows the average tenure to be 4.2 years, a difference of approximately two months – hardly worth mentioning as a major trend in the employment landscape.

Employees want career guidance, but they also want skills growth. Our talent mobility research has uncovered a variety of companies that have somewhat radical approaches to growing and managing their workforce, from allowing employees to pick up and move across the organizational chart to a manager they feel is more likely to support their developmental needs, to firms that offer stretch assignments with very clear goals and outcomes as a way to create value for individuals, teams and the business. The challenge is that while many employers want to participate in these types of programmes, they are not sure how to make them a reality. The leap from theory to application can be considerably difficult because of potential conflicts with culture and organizational norms. The Lighthouse Research Talent Mobility Profit Chain in Figure 1.1 shows a high-level overview of how these talent practices relate to the results of the business.

This need for growth is partially driven by the widely recognized skills gap. Research from Udemy,[10] a learning technology platform, shows that 80 per cent of Americans believe there is a skills gap, and this number is fairly consistent globally. Additionally, 35 per cent of American workers say that the skills gap affects them personally. Within the study, respondents said that they expected the responsibility for reskilling the workforce to fall on the shoulders not only of individuals and businesses, but of governments as well. The participants in the research also said that the skills areas they most need to

Figure 1.1   Lighthouse Research Talent Mobility Profit Chain

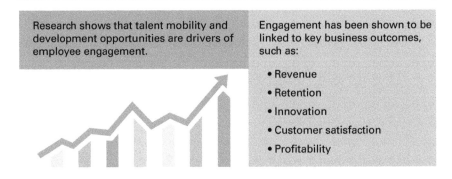

Research shows that talent mobility and development opportunities are drivers of employee engagement.

Engagement has been shown to be linked to key business outcomes, such as:

- Revenue
- Retention
- Innovation
- Customer satisfaction
- Profitability

focus on (from most to least important) include technology skills, leadership and management, productivity skills, interpersonal work skills and soft skills.

Learning agility

Taking the previous discussion into the employer's hands, businesses need to be looking at how to train and teach workers in a way that improves the firm's overall agility in the marketplace. Training is about more than just safety – it's a way to continuously invest in the success of the organization over time. One area we'll focus on shortly is the concept of the 'employee experience', which translates to the learner experience in this context. In the course of research for a project on informal learning tools and measurement, I spoke with a global learning and development leader about the idea of the learner experience. His response surprised me at the time, but in hindsight it is very appropriate. He said that the whole idea of creating a positive, friendly experience for learners was a complete waste of resources and time if the intent was only to create that type of experience. However, if creating that positive experience led to other benefits, such as increased learner engagement, retention of materials, or performance, then it was a valuable process in which he'd be more than happy to invest his training budget. In other words, the experience can't be the outcome; it has to lead to a worthwhile outcome.

At the same time, employers are faced with a decision about how and where to invest their learning budgets in a high-impact manner. Technology plays a part, and we'll dig into the AI applications for learning and development later in the book, but core components like training and learning content are also important to how learning gets accomplished within an organization. Our research shows that high-performing employers are more likely to look at learning content for the engagement value it creates. For those companies, value comes in the form of voluntary consumption and adoption rates, not just considering quantity of content development or course completions as the ultimate goal of the learning and development function. It's about quality more than quantity in this case. Low performers are seven times more likely to say their learning content does not engage learners or is merely transactional in nature (Lighthouse Research, 2017).[11] This may be due to the starting and ending points: the strategy around creation and measurement. Many companies are not using a comprehensive strategy to guide their learning objectives, yet we all know that it's impossible to hit a target if we don't first aim at it. Employers that try to use learning as a differentiator for creating a more valuable workforce are doomed to fail if their approach is purely ad hoc. Filling skills gaps on a first-come, first-served basis means that L&D teams will always struggle to keep up with demand. Taking a more strategic approach and prioritizing content development and delivery based on business objectives is more likely to lead to high-impact learning programmes, which is why high performers are twice as likely to have a strategy leading their learning investments and activities.

And this overview could easily go on, delving into any number of areas from analytics and onboarding to workforce management and engagement. The world is becoming more complex, not less, and employers need to seize the current opportunity where there is more data and insight than ever before on hand to help solve the problems that exist. One area that offers promise in solving those problems is

Figure 1.2   Approach to learning content strategy

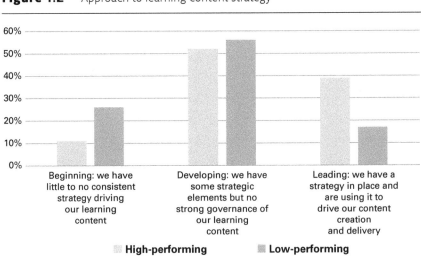

SOURCE 2017 Learning Content Strategy Study, Lighthouse Research & Advisory

the employee experience, because instead of trying to treat smaller segments of the population, employers can craft a more holistic strategy for improving the workplace.

The power of the employee experience

One of the most talked about topics in all of human capital management in recent years has been the concept of the employee experience. Books, articles and presentations all tie back to this idea of creating a series of workplace experiences that create immense value for our employees. Employee engagement is a similar topic, but it's commonly seen as a subset of the broader employee experience and engagement scores are used as one metric for determining the overall value of the employee experience. Any practitioner can tell you the statistics: employee engagement isn't improving and hasn't in years. Gallup's data says that about one in three employees are engaged and that number hasn't changed significantly in more than 10 years.[12] That's a key reason so many industry leaders have seen the employee experience as a potential solution to the perpetual engagement problem. Aptitude Research Partners' 2016 data shows that employers see these concepts as very similar, with 83 per cent of companies agreeing that *improving the employee experience and developing a formal engagement strategy* are their top priorities.[13] Consider the following reasons why employee experience is a must-have item on the agenda for those HR and business leaders examining workplace issues and solutions.

1 *Congruent customer and employee experiences.* How can we expect our employees to deliver superior service and customer experiences when their own experience as an employee is lacklustre or even worse? I've long said that the customer experience will never exceed the employee experience. Well, what I've actually said is, 'Employees will never treat customers better than their management treats them', but it's one and the same. The experiences will be congruent, or similar. That means companies that live and die by customer satisfaction scores need to start not

with new customer bonuses or other gimmicks but with a positive employee experience in order to see the actual outcomes they are looking for.

2 *The employee experience is not the employee lifecycle.* One of the issues with the initial attempt to grasp the concept of the employee experience is to put it in the context of the employee life cycle. Don't think that understanding the mechanics of onboarding and performance management means that you have a great employee experience. The experience, or how someone feels, is part of the life cycle, but it's not quite the same thing. Instead, look at the candidate or employee-centric nature of your processes and see to what extent they support, encourage and engage your workforce. That's how you can get a true sense of the value you are creating through your own employee experience.

3 *Tell me about your employees first.* If I walked up to you right now and asked about your company, how would you begin the conversation? What would you start with? Your products? Your mission? Your customers? What about your employees – would they even make it into the discussion? I once asked this question of several dozen business leaders as an experiment and not a single one of them responded to me with a description of their employees or the kinds of people they hire. It's so common to think about this question in the context of customers or services when in reality it's our employees that make us successful. Start the discussion with employees as your central topic and go from there. It will change the perspective of those around you.

4 *Expectations rule the day.* A big part of why employees have bad experiences in the workplace is expectations. Have you ever had high expectations for a raise, performance discussion or meeting, only to walk away feeling disappointed? Or maybe your first few days on the job are a complete waste of time, sitting around waiting for resources, despite being treated very positively in the hiring process? The theory of expectancy plays into motivations and how we feel about choices we make. If you want to deliver a positive experience, make sure you give people a warning ahead of time so

their expectation gap (what they expect and what you ultimately deliver) isn't as large.

5 *Companies don't really exist, people do.* The trouble with leaders in many organizations is that they view the company as 'The Company', an autonomous entity that doesn't need to be understood or afforded respect. In this worldview, decisions are made as if employees are replacement parts, and we don't have to worry about the feelings of replaceable parts. This is exemplified by the way one company manages its workforce. A popular ride-sharing company actually uses an algorithm to assign shifts and communicate with workers, which has led to drivers cheating the system in order to improve their own financial outcomes. This story is highlighted more fully later in the book, but the key element to remember is that companies can't assume that people are emotionless automatons, because they aren't. People get stuff done, not 'the company'. People are the face of the firm, not a logo, billboard, or slogan. Remember that.

6 *Success results from design thinking.* The concept of design thinking centres on this; efforts are spent not just on solving problems, but on creating solutions with the end result in mind. In this case, how can we create solutions that focus not on the organization or solely on the customer, but on the employee experience. Instead of thinking about how to fix a problem specifically, the focus is on becoming something radically different. For many of us, that's the direction we need to go to rectify design flaws in our processes and policies that can actually hamper our efforts to engage our workers. For instance, in a recent interview with an HR executive, she explained that the company had done away with the normal 'doctor's note for sick leave' requirement. She said that when someone gets a cold, they would respond in one of a few ways; sending them to the doctor to get a piece of paper even when the doctor could not improve their condition often made them angry or upset, and other workers would continue coming to work even with a cold because they didn't want the hassle of scheduling a doctor's appointment in the middle of their

illness. This is a small example of how HR leaders can look for ways to design processes and approaches that support employee needs first and business needs second, because in reality taking care of employees is how you take care of the business.

The new normal: doing more with less

These and other talent-specific challenges are facing HR leaders around the world every day, and that's not all. On top of this we have the constant barrage from the business to 'do more with less'. This is a reality and has been for some time for many companies. Of the various areas of the business, this concept seems to hit human resources harder than many others. For example, a 1–100 ratio is commonly seen as the 'standard' ratio of HR staff to employees, yet if that ratio shifts to 1–1,000, there is virtually no time for that HR staff member to participate in anything even remotely strategic. All efforts are spent on day-to-day activities, shuffling paper and other administrative work. Even if none of these other shifts and challenges were present, this one would still remain as an incredible barrier to HR leaders being able to deliver high-value service to both the employer and the employee population.

When we combine the leanness of today's HR teams with the need to create more personalized experiences for workers, we have a perfect storm of demands that simply can't be met in the traditional manner. All this is not meant to show that HR can't overcome these challenges. With the right tools, we absolutely can. Consider the consumer examples of how technology enables highly personalized experiences at scale. ESPN relaunched its website properties, allowing users to specify which sports or teams they are interested in. This gives each individual a highly customized experience from the exact moment they visit the website. Our mobile devices allow us to set up specific applications and options in ways that make us more productive, and no two people have the same exact settings and preferences because no two people are exactly the same. While simple, these examples provide a hint at the value that technology can provide in the workplace as well, by creating highly personalized experiences regardless of whether the audience is a candidate, a line-level employee or a business leader. For instance, one example we'll explore in a coming chapter shows how a recruiting technology provider created an interface that allows candidates to have conversations with a humanized chatbot, focusing in on their most relevant experience and interests just as a human interviewer might in the screening process. This isn't just about automating that workload, which has its own inherent value – it's also about creating that personalized feeling for those who interact with these sorts of systems so that they feel appreciated and understood.

Leveraging new technologies can bring about myriad improvements in employer operations, and the core of many new technologies is some variety of artificial intelligence. While AI may conjure up images of robots and movie plots, the type of AI discussed here is more benign. It's less physical and more technical. It's less about general-purpose AI, which doesn't exist outside of a science fiction movie, and more about leveraging automation and other capabilities of AI for highly specialized data sets, predictions and outcomes. The discussion of artificial intelligence today often centres around two key areas that we'll explore more deeply in the coming chapters: automation and augmentation. The intent is to truly do more with less, freeing up our high-value HR talent to pursue more strategic activities and letting the algorithms do the repetitive heavy lifting and analysis.

Exercise: thinking beyond today

If you're like most business leaders, today has been busy. It's been challenging. You've spent some time on things that may or may not have been on your formal 'to do' list, which might mean you're farther behind today than you were when you started. It's important occasionally to rise above this general busyness and think beyond the day. For the moment, put yourself in the place of an entrepreneur running your own organization or department. Think about the resources at your disposal, the tasks you have to get done, and the value of your time. Oftentimes employees, even executives, have trouble thinking about the specific value of their time, but entrepreneurs are often better at realizing what is a core focus area and what needs to be outsourced or delegated. With that in mind, if you had an additional hour in your day, how would you spend it? What would you *spend it on*, or more importantly, what would you *invest it in*? Take a moment and write down two or three things you would do with that extra time. Would you brush up on professional development needs? Would you refine some of your processes around gathering and reporting metrics? Maybe you'd do personal phone calls to more candidates instead of sending mass e-mails? Whatever the case, each of us has different priorities, so consider yours for a moment.

A more personal example of this is a personal budget for someone with irregular income. It's challenging to budget month-to-month with an irregular income, so financial planners often recommend an irregular income planning process that lists priorities from most to least important. As money comes into the household, individuals start applying it to the top of the list and moving down the priorities. At the top of the list might be groceries or utilities, and near the bottom would be discretionary spending on areas you care about. This concept is the same as our discussion on how you'd spend additional time but helps to make it more concrete because there is a prioritized list that governs how additional resources are applied as they become available.

This exercise is important because the promise of artificial intelligence tools is, at its core, more time. By automating a part of HR and having an algorithm or machine handle the work, it frees us up to do other things. The problem with this is Parkinson's Law. Parkinson's Law states that our work task will expand to fill the time available. In reality, when we have a new innovation that 'adds' time to our day by reducing some administrative requirement, the rest of our work creeps into that available time in an unobtrusive way, eliminating that saving if we're not careful. The problem is that time creep happens based on urgency or some other criteria instead of coming from a strategic look at the high-value actions that generate the most value for the person, the team or the company. One final example of this: if an HR leader earns $50 an hour and a new tool saves that person an hour a week, the benefit to the company isn't just the $50 per week in saved time – it should also include the new, higher-value activity the HR leader is pursuing with that freed-up time.

The coming chapters will include case studies that show greater automation and time savings. They will tell about revolutionary technologies and tools that promise to improve the workplace. But if we don't think critically about how we'll use that additional time saved from automation, then we're leaving a large portion of the value on the table. As you proceed through the book, be thinking very clearly about how these advancements might apply to your own organization and how you might use those additional hours to improve your own standing, credibility and value.

Using this book

If it hasn't happened already, one day a business leader at your company will come to you and ask about the impact that artificial intelligence will have on the HR function. It's my hope that this book will help you to answer that question both on a macro scale (how artificial intelligence impacts the HR profession and the competencies necessary for success) and the micro scale (how this impacts your company and your HR team).

What good is a tool if it's presented in theory only? This book will help you not only understand the concept of AI as a technology, but more importantly, you will understand the use cases and opportunities for HR to adopt these tools and systems to support our ever-present quest for improving business outcomes through better people practices.

The best way to accomplish this is not by looking at HR as a giant mishmash of practices and processes. That sort of viewpoint is exactly why general-purpose AI is more of a buzzword than an actual application of practical value today. Instead, we will examine HR through discrete practice areas such as recruiting and talent acquisition, learning and development, talent management and more. This book is designed to help you become a better professional, pure and simple. If you're hoping to get a more general idea of how AI works and how it is penetrating every part of our lives, Chapter 2 will be beneficial to you. If you are more interested in a specific use case, there are chapters dedicated to answering your questions around items such as payroll (Chapter 3), recruiting (Chapter 5) or learning (Chapter 6).

In addition, there are challenges with these types of technology, just like any other. With that in mind, this analysis will also examine some of the more common challenges with using artificial intelligence, such as system bias. We will also focus on the competencies that matter most for an HR leader in a digital world, requiring a mixture of human ingenuity and creativity with the scalability and insight that machines can provide. This balance has always been a challenge since the earliest days of automation, but in a world where knowledge work rules and computers are doing an increasing amount of knowledge work, the discussion is more pertinent than ever.

Key points

- Today's world of HR is more complex than ever before, and a disruptive environment requires companies to be more agile in order to respond to market demands.

- Talent acquisition, learning, workforce management and other core HR practice areas are all affected by changes in candidate and employee preferences, which places even greater demand on today's HR function.

- Employee experience is more than a buzzword – it's a way to encapsulate the entire sum of experiences that employees perceive from the first application through to the last touch of offboarding. Employers must ask themselves if those moments, either in whole or in part, are generating positive experiences for their candidates and employees.

- New artificial intelligence technologies that automate and augment the workforce could be the key to solving some of the thorny issues and increased demands for HR to accomplish more with fewer resources.

Notes

1 http://www-935.ibm.com/services/c-suite/study/studies/chro-study/

2 http://www.wsj.com/articles/is-uber-a-friend-or-foe-of-carnegie-mellon-in-robotics-1433084582

3 http://money.cnn.com/2016/05/06/news/economy/gig-economy-princeton-krueger-tiny/

4 https://www.usatoday.com/story/money/business/2013/08/22/ten-largest-employers/2680249/

5 http://lhra.io/blog/business-value-hr-technology-research-preview/

6 http://lhra.io/blog/todays-top-talent-acquisition-priorities-free-ebook/

7 http://lhra.io/blog/global-hr-practices-compliance-growth-productivity-new-research/

8 https://www.bls.gov/opub/mlr/1984/10/art2full.pdf

9 https://www.bls.gov/news.release/tenure.nr0.htm

10 https://research.udemy.com/research_report/2017-skills-gap-report/

11 http://lhra.io/blog/new-research-radically-rethinking-learning-content-strategy-free-report/

12 http://news.gallup.com/businessjournal/188033/worldwide-employee-engagement-crisis.aspx

13 http://lhra.io/blog/value-employee-experience-free-ebook/

The basics of artificial intelligence

Between 14 and 21 million lives. That's how many people are estimated to have been saved by the codebreaking genius of Alan Turing and his team. Known as the father of modern computing, Alan Turing was a brilliant mathematician who dedicated his time during World War II to breaking codes and ciphers. During the conflict, one of the most challenging tasks undertaken by the British military was to break the codes used by the Axis powers in order to understand troop movements, attack plans and other important information. Perhaps the most difficult coding technology in the world at the time was known as Enigma, the system used by the Germans. After some time and an extensive amount of effort, a team of British codebreakers were able to crack Enigma. In an analysis of the data, researchers estimate that cracking the Enigma code using a system designed by Turing led to shortening the war by several years, saving millions of lives in the process (Copeland, 2012).[1]

Note: the goal for this chapter is to be as short as possible so you can move on to the more practical elements of this book while still being long enough to help you understand how the data analysis and artificial intelligence aspects of these new technologies operate. For those who have a technology background and want additional information I will share a few resources at the end of this chapter for further reading, but for those who are hoping to see how this truly impacts the HR profession, this will carry you right into Chapter 3, where we really start delving into specific examples of technologies and use cases for human capital management (HCM).

What does this have to do with artificial intelligence? One of Turing's other contributions based on his mathematical research was the concept of a 'thinking machine' (Sharkey, 2012).[2] Turing envisioned a machine that could think like a human and even proposed an experiment, called a Turing Test, to determine if a machine could pass as a human. The Turing Test is a process where an interrogator interacts with a person and a machine via an electronic interface and then has to guess which is the human and which is the machine. In order to pass the Turing Test, a machine has to be able to passably simulate a human level of intelligence in the short duration of the examination. In spite of the tragic loss of Alan Turing before his time, his name is regularly referenced today with regard to artificial intelligence because of his significant early contributions to the field of research.

While the stakes are lower than those associated with codebreaking during wartime, the technologies we use today in the workplace are still incredibly important. Over the years I have seen hundreds of technologies, analysed their functionality and advised businesses on how to develop their products and market approaches. The reason they seek this advice is partly because I bring a practitioner's viewpoint to the conversation, helping them to think about product development from their buyer's mindset. When I'm looking at a piece of technology, I think about my time working as an HR executive and ask myself the question, 'Would this have made my life easier in a practical way, or is it more flash than substance?' It's a challenging lens because not all software meets that threshold of 'practical value', but it's important if someone wants to serve an audience of HR and business leaders to be clear about the value the system can bring to the stakeholders. The other reason vendors seek advice is because I have researched and analysed trends in the HR and learning technology industries. While there's no way to intimately know and stay connected with all the providers in the industry, doing several briefings and product demos every week keeps me fresh on the latest advancements and directions of key providers. This insight into technology offerings matters, since a product conversation rarely occurs these days without a mention of machine learning, algorithms, or other AI-based concepts. It's possible you've also seen a demo, heard a sales pitch or read about a vendor's technology that relies on artificial intelligence to operate. This chapter will help to give you the essential grounding in AI technologies in plain terms, making the conversation as practical as possible and helping you to cut through the marketing language and understand just how a particular system leverages AI to operate. Or, as often happens, you'll be able to see through the hype and understand when someone might be overinflating the capabilities of their particular system.

I've already established my intent to make this book highly practical and actionable for you, which requires a knowledge of application, not just theory. The best way to understand how we arrived at this intersection of artificial intelligence and the human resources profession is to take a step back and look at the logical progression of things over time. AI tools such as machine learning require immense amounts of data – millions of data points – to be successful. Not surprisingly, the business buzzword of recent years has been 'big data', which is a foundational underpinning of a system powered by artificial intelligence. Without the improvements in data creation and capture in recent history, there would be no opportunity to utilize AI to drive predictive models. By gathering the necessary amount of data, we can then predict trends, outcomes and more by understanding the variables. Additionally, research from Sierra-Cedar's report explores a category of firms called talent-driven organizations, those that use analytics to solve key talent challenges around engagement, retention and identification of top talent. The research finds that talent-driven organizations are much more likely to have machine learning-driven business intelligence and HR analytics tools in place. These types of firms are 166 per cent more likely to be using these systems and 68 per cent more likely to be evaluating new systems to solve the problems associated with talent analytics.[3] That data point helps to demonstrate why this discussion matters, so consider the following 'layperson's' definition of predictive analytics to help lay the groundwork for the exploration of AI that is to come.

A layperson's guide to predictive HR analytics

One of the challenges of talking about predictive analytics, big data and other similar concepts is that it quickly becomes both complex and abstract, causing the general audience to tune out the conversation. This is especially relevant for HR leaders, where competencies in these areas are somewhat weak in general. By the way, that's not an indictment on HR leaders, it's just a statement of the facts. That's not to say they aren't great leaders or don't have the skills and experience necessary to work within the HCM field. It's just that the need to gather, analyse and predict outcomes using data has not been a required skill set for very long.

I had a conversation with a technology firm founder that talked about some of the work he had done supporting NASA and other government technology projects over the years. He said that an interesting shift happened over time. In earlier decades, the focus was mainly on hardware, and software was a very minor component. Systems were built out of 'dumb' parts and had a very limited number of computers and other technology to support their operation. Over time, the software element increased exponentially both in power and in impact as technology improved. There was a time somewhere in the middle of this ongoing transition where some hardware engineers had to 'become' software engineering subject matter experts. While this group of individuals might not have had formal training or education in software systems, the workers had the right understanding of the programs, customers and objectives that a newly trained software engineer out of college wouldn't have. Their limitations on the technical side didn't hamper their ability to add value to the rest of the process.

I see the same thing happening today within HR. In recent years we've felt the need to turn HR leaders into analytics experts, even though that might not be their core skill set. Whether you are an expert or brand new to the topic of HR analytics, I want to help you understand the impact of analytics and how they work. My goal is to transform you not into an expert able to carry out analyses and perform statistical modelling, but into a more conscious and educated participant when it comes to those analytics and data conversations I mentioned previously. Let's start with a quick overview of the three types of analytics (Table 2.1) before jumping into the conversation around the predictive analytics that can be generated by many of the machine learning tools today.

Table 2.1 Types of talent analytics

Analytics type	Purpose	Example
Descriptive	Tells current state	Retention rate
Predictive	Correlates data points to predict changes	Personalized retention predictions
Prescriptive	Suggests potential solutions to predicted changes	Personalized retention suggestions

What are predictive analytics?

In the book *Predictive HR Analytics: Mastering the HR metric* (Edwards and Edwards, 2016, Kogan Page), the authors talk about three specific ways to discuss this topic:

- identifying predictors and causal factors;
- predictive modelling; *Best use for TA*
- predicting behaviours.

Again, the goal is to present this in laymen's terms, so let's dive in.

Concept 1: identifying predictors and causal factors

In this instance, we are trying to find out what variables are linked to each other. Data can be tied together by correlation or causation. Correlation simply means that there seems to be a relationship in the data (for example, people seem to carry umbrellas more often when rain is predicted). Causation is something else entirely (for example, we know that carrying an umbrella does not cause it to rain more frequently).

   If we can identify what variables feed into others, then we can use those drivers or levers to create the results we need. For instance, if we can link increased training to higher sales, then that would seem to be a causal factor. Testing would need to be done to determine the extent of the linkage, but you get the picture. The first, most basic step for prediction is finding those predictors. Then we build on top of that foundation.

Concept 2: predictive modelling

This takes the conversation a step further. Let me clarify really quickly – we are talking here about leading variables. When a leading variable changes, it affects other elements down the line. Think about it like an assembly line – if we change something on the front end, the rest of the process is affected dramatically. If we mess up on the front end, then the rest of the process is affected in a different way. That's how we use leading variables within the predictive conversation.

Once we have identified the predictor variables from the previous section, we step up a notch and start trying to predict what happens if we change one of our predictor variables. For instance, if we continue with the training/sales link mentioned above, the goal might be to try and see if doubling training also doubles sales. Or, in another context, maybe we find out that there is a link between manager communication and employee engagement. Then we start trying to model whether increasing or decreasing manager communications affects engagement and to what extent. The point here is to focus on the driver variables and determine what happens if we start changing them around. How do they impact the final result? What changes occur?

Concept 3: predicting behaviours

The final and most complex piece is determining what happens if we apply our model to new data or populations. In other words, can we predict how people will respond to certain variables?

Let's say we have data on employee turnover that is related to a variety of factors, including manager check-ins, performance evaluation scores and tenure. By mapping all of those variables for existing employees, we can create a model that will allow us to predict future behaviours. For instance, if the data shows that fewer manager check-ins, shorter tenure and lower performance scores indicate someone is more likely to leave, we can put that person in a 'high risk' bucket. The person is more likely to leave than someone that doesn't have those types of factors working against them.

Another example could be around recruiting. Let's say that inter-view teams of five or more people have been proven to screen better employees with higher performance than teams of four or fewer interviewers. With the right data behind the model that proves this relationship, we can make the case that having five interviewers, while a fairly significant investment of time, is a good trade-off for improved employee performance for the duration of employment. The next step, of course, would be to quantify the improved performance and how much value it ultimately derives for the organization. As you can see, there's incredible power in leveraging large amounts of data, which is a core component of how AI tools function. Now, let's examine the level of artificial intelligence development and market penetration as it stands in today's market.

Artificial intelligence components

AI is a topic that is bandied about more often today than ever before, yet it's often completely misunderstood. While robots and systems that act without regular human inputs do indeed exist, many newer tools are based on more rudimentary elements of AI, not self-aware, intelligent machines that learn from every interaction. The term 'artificial intelligence' is actually an overarching category with several more targeted terms falling under that heading, including:

- machine learning;
- natural language processing;
- deep learning;
- neural networks.

Each of these individual technologies is powerful, but when combined they create opportunities to eliminate wasted time, improve productivity and drive better results. But before we dive into how these technologies work, it is helpful to understand some of the fundamental components.

The definition of artificial intelligence

If your hopes of what AI can achieve are based on science fiction movies, then you'll probably be somewhat disappointed to learn that many technologies today are not yet artificially intelligent to the degree we might hope or expect. Even as early as the 1950s researchers expected to have artificially intelligent systems in place by the year 2000, but this didn't occur as they expected. It's important to see artificial intelligence as a *spectrum*, not as a single *destination*. For example, any physics student with a graphing calculator has use of an advanced piece of technology that automates equations and processes data faster than the average human. Does that qualify as an AI system? Systems and tools like this may perform repetitive functions or automate a specific task, but that doesn't necessarily reflect the full promise AI has to offer. To establish a definition, let's consider what true AI looks like from Oxford's English Dictionary:[4]

> The capacity of a computer to perform operations analogous to learning and decision making in humans.

While we could spend time debating the definition of AI and what it means, I prefer to take the same viewpoint as one of the most influential and ambitious research efforts around artificial intelligence, the Stanford One Hundred Year Study on Artificial Intelligence (AI100). The AI100's definition of AI points out the fact that a lack of a highly precise and universally embraced definition of AI is one of the key reasons for the explosive growth in the field (Stone *et al*, 2016).[5] The general sense of pursuing a human-like level of processing and perception is enough to drive the field of research and uncover practical applications.

In more plain language, artificially intelligent systems have to not only analyse activities and predict outcomes – they also need to learn from those predictions over time. The actual analysis and prediction is relatively easy. Software companies have been able to do that for years, and the technology is fairly stable. IBM's Watson is a great example of a technology that makes millions of predictions a day on everything from which employees are going to leave the organization all the way to examining medical images to determine if patients have cancer. A great resource on this topic of predictions is *Prediction Machines*, a book that explores the economic impacts of increasingly cheaper prediction capabilities offered by today's technology. Through an economics lens, if predictions are cheaper, they should be more plentiful. Lower cost leads to greater supply, whether that is a supply of fruit, vehicles or even predictions. If these predictions are more plentiful, then we can use them in a wide variety of applications. This proliferation of predictions is already a reality today, as you'll see with some of the applications we'll explore in the coming pages.

The challenge for most AI technologies comes in the *learning* aspect. Intelligence at a human level is based on constant surveying of information, learning from that information, and adjusting decisions accordingly. It's always been that way. In the early days, when a caveman was eaten by a sabre-toothed tiger, his neighbour watched and decided (wisely) to avoid those animals in the future. That's the essential component of intelligence. In organizational development terms we call this 'informal learning', or learning that occurs in the everyday course of life and work. In contrast, formal learning is intentional training delivered with the expectation of improving intelligence or performance. Informal learning comes naturally to humans and is something we can do with relative ease, yet it's more challenging for computers to grasp the nuances of every situation.

An interesting concept that relates to this idea of how machines learn is Moravec's paradox (Rotenberg, 2017).[6] The core element of the paradox is that scientists can teach machines to do difficult or complex tasks like playing chess or solving algebra equations, yet they can't replicate the capabilities of a toddler to recognize faces, walk across a room, or associate words with items they see. One possible cause for the paradox outlined by Hans Moravec is evolution. Over time, humans have learned and mastered critical skills that seem effortless to us, such as walking or comprehending speech. Moravec posed the idea that the older the skill, the longer it will take to reverse-engineer it for purposes of recreating it with software. Strangely, skills that are more difficult for humans to grasp, such as geometry or calculus, are more easily programmed into a computer's capabilities.

If you read any headlines today, you might see some of the more vocal opponents of AI talking about how the systems and tools in place are not really 'intelligent'. There's actually a name for this phenomenon: the AI Effect (Bailey, 2016).[7] In essence, once a machine is able to demonstrate a human process or capability, onlookers dismiss it as an advance in computational power or computer modelling, not as an advance in machine intelligence. For instance, these were the claims when IBM's computer was able to beat the world's best chess player. Noted computer scientist and mathematician Larry Tesler is known for saying, 'Intelligence is whatever machines haven't done yet.'[8] Once a machine has done a task, we cease to think of it as intelligence and instead see it as something else, such as statistical modelling. While it must be frustrating for AI developers and computer scientists to face this reality, from a practical standpoint *it doesn't change the results*. I'll say it again: whether it's 'intelligence' or not doesn't matter if it achieves the intended result. Intelligence can be just as much of a philosophical or theological discussion as a technological one. If a computer can perform a task that a human could perform, that falls somewhere on the spectrum of artificial intelligence.

This general pushback on the definition of intelligence is due to what Tesler believes is an innate human desire to be different and unique. After all, if we have a computer that can copy what we do as humans, that makes us less unique in the world, right? However, as you'll see throughout this book and particularly in the chapter on future-proofing your skills, that doesn't necessarily have to ring true. There are plenty of capabilities humans have that robots and algorithms can't easily match. Think of it this way: when Microsoft turned the full power of its web services toward translating Wikipedia's three billion words across 5 million articles from English to another language at its Ignite event in 2016, that translation occurred in less than one second.[9] However, despite that translation and all the raw power at their disposal, the systems can't call you on the phone and have a half-hour conversation with you. There is still a large gap between the capabilities of today's technologies and the very human nature of life and work.

I agree that 'general AI' doesn't really exist today in the form of a machine that can mimic a wide range of human abilities, but there are plenty of opportunities to leverage more specific, targeted solutions. While a computer might not be able to quickly learn how to brush teeth, cook breakfast and drive to work, different systems and applications might be able to analyse your dental records to find cavities, examine a photo of your breakfast and estimate the calories, or offer route alternatives for your commute based on current traffic reports and data. These are just a few of millions of potential applications for artificial intelligence to improve our lives in a variety of ways. However, for computers to get better at making predictions and actually learning from the data over time, they require immense amounts of data in order to accurately process information. This isn't about looking through one hundred or even one thousand data points to train an algorithm. It takes exponentially more.

Consider the example of the 2012 experiment at Google where engineer Andrew Ng worked to teach a computer to understand if an image included a cat or not. Consider that for a moment. This would be an easy task for virtually any child to complete – simply look at the photo and determine if a cat is present in the photo or not. While it seems like a simple premise, the setup required images from more than 10 million videos in order to adequately and accurately train the system to recognize cats within photos with any measure of accuracy (Markoff, 2012).[10]

While it's easier to mention AI in marketing hype than it is to leverage it in practice, there are some technology providers that stand out from the pack with rigorous approaches, complex algorithms and a strong focus on improving the lives of HR professionals with intuitive technology. There is no shortage of software companies pointing to their use of artificial intelligence, but how many of them are really solving problems with the tools they're developing?

The following definitions are provided as a tool to help readers ensure that they grasp some of the more nuanced applications and uses for various aspects of artificial intelligence. They provide a foundation of understanding for the discussion around specific applications of AI in the workplace, from matching candidates to jobs to predicting what kinds of training might be best for an employee's development plan.

Machine learning

Machine learning (ML) is a type of AI that provides computers with the ability to learn without being explicitly programmed. The problem with computers historically is that they can complete a task, but then their 'mind' resets and you have to start from scratch if you need them to repeat that task again. Machine learning works by examining large sets of data and uses patterns in that data to improve a program's own understanding. In traditional machine learning, the learning process is supervised and the programmer has to be very specific when telling the computer what types of things it should be looking for when deciding based on past known outcomes. For instance, the programmer might explicitly tell the algorithm where to find new data inputs, how to compute them and what to take action on. In advanced machine learning, unsupervised algorithms learn from inference and not the programmer. This is when things truly get interesting, because computers might see themes or other important factors that humans simply can't comprehend, and in supervised machine learning the programmer might not take those factors into consideration. With an unsupervised algorithm, the system can return all relevant, interesting data points for consideration before adjusting itself. While this is a neat idea, it's not yet a reality for the most part. Today virtually all *commercially viable* machine learning applications use supervised learning. As mentioned previously, the learning element is the critical component. Many of the technologies laid out in this book depend heavily on this aspect of artificial intelligence as a foundational element of success. When machine learning truly becomes unsupervised, it creates opportunities for greater learning and understanding to occur.

Many large businesses are making headway in leveraging machine learning. In a 2015 meeting, Google CEO, Sundar Pichai, said, 'Machine learning is a core, transformative way by which we're re-thinking everything we're doing' (Niccolai, 2015).[11] For a firm like Google, this means every data point the company captures across its products is used to guide and develop new capabilities and enhance others. For instance, the more than two trillion annual searches in Google's world-renowned search engine, clicking activities across the company's global advertising network, and even how users interact with Gmail all factor into the algorithms that seek to understand the human population. The same goes for other Google-level technology competitors such as Facebook, IBM, Microsoft and others. Each of the firms, in its own way, is looking for ways to capitalize on the advancements machine learning offers.

Clearly, machine learning has a multitude of applications and many more that are yet to be defined. Some highly specialized forms of machine learning are available today in the consumer context. For instance, your video streaming service might suggest movies that you will enjoy based on previous viewing patterns and ratings. Or your favourite e-commerce platform might be able to predict what products you might like to buy based on a combination of your past purchases, items you've explored in a search engine and what others with similar buying behaviours typically seek. These are commonplace and actually anticipated by consumers, and each relies on a large amount of data to ensure their operation and accuracy of predictions.

Natural language processing

Natural language processing (NLP) is a fundamental element of artificial intelligence. For machines to interact with humans, they must understand how humans interact with other humans. In virtually every case, that interaction is either written or verbal. Natural language processing is the ability of a computer to understand human language as it is spoken – the 'natural' part is essential. In order for a system to understand human speech or text, it requires large inputs to train and teach the system on what humans sound like. Natural language processing algorithms are based on machine learning where interpretation can be made from data that can be ambiguous, like spoken languages typically are. Additional elements other than the specific words, such as context, tone and structures in the data, can be interpreted by the computer during the process. Instead of hand-coding large sets of rules for how to read and understand speech, natural language processing can rely on machine learning to automatically learn these rules by analysing large sets of examples.

NLP is commonly used today for a variety of tasks in our everyday needs. One element of NLP that has promising applications is not just the processing of the inputs but the recommendation of outputs through automated question answering. For instance, the newest version of Android's stock Messenger application can read a text from someone and suggest a handful of potential responses in order to speed up the conversation. If someone sends you a text reading, 'How about dinner tonight?', the application may offer up options such as, 'Sounds good', or 'Yes', or 'Maybe later'. Because NLP consumes large amounts of data, it can already begin predicting potential responses to questions with some measure of accuracy.

Some of the other use cases for natural language processing include text mining, speech tagging and parsing, translation, sentiment analysis and speech recognition. Text mining is a process of analysing text data for trends and other insights. For employers, this might mean seeing a list of keywords or phrases in your Glassdoor profile that illuminate how candidates and employees see your company and its culture based on open text reviews, comments and ratings. Translation is another obvious value point. In the past translation required a paid translator and additional time for translation. While the output isn't 100 per cent accurate at this time, online tools can translate many languages instantly as you type. One final example to explore is sentiment analysis. Sentiment analysis is the process of looking at large chunks of unstructured data, such as a sampling of correspondence from a company's e-mail server, and determining the overall sentiment or mood of the population based on that sampling. The process works by analysing word use and tone and extrapolating to determine the perceived mood of the senders. We will explore this concept more fully in the next chapter as there are tools available today to offer this value to employers – the main purpose here is to show the value natural language processing can bring to the workplace.

Deep learning

Deep learning is the next step and possibly the most critical aspect on the AI continuum where machines begin creating true artificial intelligence. At its most basic level, deep learning can be thought of as a series of machine learning decisions where outputs from one decision inform the analysis of the next. At its core, human learning is a set of processes that continuously sort through complex abstractions by building a hierarchy in which each sequential level is created with knowledge that was gained from the preceding layer of the hierarchy. For instance, if you are shown a photo of an animal, you start filtering it automatically and subconsciously without even thinking:

- Does it have fur, scales, or feathers? Fur.
- What colour is it? Black.
- What is it? Cat.

The same process happens on a computational level in deep learning where algorithms are stacked in a hierarchy of increasing complexity and abstraction, mimicking the human learning processes. Computer programs that use deep learning go through much of the same learning process. Iterations continue until the output reaches an acceptable level of accuracy. The number of data processing layers necessary for the process is what inspired the term 'deep' in deep learning. Not only is deep learning fast, it is usually highly accurate. In order to achieve a higher level of accuracy than machine learning, deep learning programs require access to immense amounts of training data and processing power, neither of which were easily available to programmers until the era of big data and cloud computing. Additionally, deep learning programming is able to compare, analyse, create and comprehend unstructured data.

Use cases today for deep learning include many types of big data analytics like language translation, medical diagnosis, stock market trading signals, network security and image identification. On example of this in action is image identification, or computer vision. This is the process of teaching a computer to understand what is in an image. The experiment mentioned earlier in this chapter by Andrew Ng is a great example of how this works in practice. By teaching a system how to 'see' a cat within an image, it became increasingly good at discerning whether a cat was present in an image, regardless of whether it was being held by a person, was partially obscured by an object, or had some other distractor element in the image. Cats are one thing, but it's worth noting that this underlying technology has a wide variety of applications. For instance, as companies continue to work on the development of self-driving cars, one critical aspect will be the identification of street signs and signals and both vehicular and foot traffic. Just like with human drivers, self-driving cars will have mere fractions of a second to calculate whether a red light is showing or a pedestrian has stepped into the street.

Neural networks

To scale deep learning, neural networks are the next step in the complexity of artificial intelligence. A neural network is a system of hardware and/or software loosely patterned after the operation of neurons in the human brain. Within a human brain, there can be billions of neurons that guide behaviours, impact learning capability and more. Artificial neural networks are a variety of deep learning technologies and operate by filtering decisions through a matrix of layered calculations before arriving at an answer. Importantly, these systems contain a learning element where they improve outputs over time. The most common is the delta rule, where delta stands for the range between the correct response and the successive responses prior to it. In plain terms, a neural network is presented with a problem and it makes a simple guess as to the answer, then it factors in the delta and adjusts its algorithms with each following calculation to get closer approximations to the correct answer. These calculations happen rapidly, and once the neural network has been trained it can serve as an analytical tool for other data.

Commercial applications of these technologies thus far include handwriting recognition for cheque processing, speech-to-text transcription, weather prediction and facial recognition. Facial recognition is the one that most of us are familiar with, as both Google Photos and Facebook have the capability to tell who is in a given set of photos. If you upload a picture to your Facebook profile, it can usually automatically tag your friends in the photo because it has mapped their faces and recognizes them in the image. I'll repeat my earlier statement: while this sounds like a relatively simple task for a human, it requires intense power and amounts of data for computers to learn to accomplish it. For example, what if only half the face is on the screen? What if the person is wearing a hat? What if the person has a very close relative that looks similar? In order to determine who a person is in a given photo, the algorithm must break down the face into its component pixels, the tiniest parts of an image, and then find similar pixel maps to compare and contrast until it finds the right person. This might be easy with a pool of 50 or 100 people, but remember that Facebook has more than 2 billion active monthly users it's always crunching data on. Impressive.

How do vendors and employers know what areas to target with AI automation?

There are dozens and dozens of specific processes and practices that exist within the HR function, and that can increase dramatically for enterprise firms, those with unique compliance requirements, or even those operating in multiple countries. So, which of those processes are best suited to being automated? Which ones are prioritized? The answer is a logical one: focus on high-volume, highly manual processes that have a high occurrence of mistakes. This set of requirements helps to clarify what employers can expect to see as machine learning algorithms continue to be leveraged for process automation.

In a research interview with Aarti Borkar, Head of Offering Management and Design for IBM's Kenexa and Watson Talent products, she explained that the company's approach to artificial intelligence applications focused not just on highly manual processes, but those that were specifically *error-prone when operated by a human*. This was a lightning bolt moment, as it helped me to understand how AI will progressively impact HR as a profession. It's not just that certain practices are more manual than others – that is a given. It's that some practices are more likely to have decision errors, mistakes, or omissions due to data velocity, volume and variety. Some examples of those processes high on the list are:

- hiring and selection;
- workforce scheduling;
- payroll.

Over time, AI applications will make their way deeper into HR process territory, but for now, several of these highlighted areas are where AI-developing firms will set their sights for the highest immediate impact and scalability.

Types of artificial intelligence technologies

Because we do not have general-purpose AI in place today, each piece of technology serves a specific purpose, such as competing in a game or responding to chat interactions. The use cases are many and varied, but it often helps to explore the various examples in order to grasp the applications and opportunities presented by artificial intelligence. More than a dozen examples have been mentioned in this chapter, some of which might have surprised you when you learned they were powered by some form of AI technology. According to a report by PitchBook, a venture capital investment analyst firm, venture capital investments in artificial intelligence technologies have exploded in recent years. The trend is up 12 times from what it was in 2008, with US $6 billion invested across more than 600 deals in 2017 (Stanfill, 2018).[12]

Additionally, Table 2.2 offers an illustration of the range of complexity that appears in artificial intelligence. The spectrum moves from broadly applicable examples to highly specialized systems, some of which you might be familiar with in your everyday life.

Table 2.2 A sampling of artificial intelligence technologies

Example	Type	Result	Technology
AstuteBot	Chatbot	Customer service bot answers questions	Natural language processing, machine learning
Alexa, Cortana, Siri	Voice-based assistants	Ask questions, get answers; over time, answers become more personalized based on activity and signals	Natural language processing, speech processing, machine learning
Microsoft Tay	Learn and imitate how humans interact online	System chats with people after they begin interacting with it	Natural language processing and machine learning

(continued)

Table 2.2 (*Continued*)

Example	Type	Result	Technology
Alibaba	Reading comprehension	Read questions, predict answers on Stanford University reading/ comprehension test	Neural network, natural language processing
Deep Dream	Replicates human brain processing	Learn as a human learns. Current project is finding and categorizing all Internet imagery	Neural network
Tesla Autopilot	Self-driving vehicle	Car that is aware of surroundings and can adjust course to avoid accidents	Machine learning

AI on a global scale

There is a tremendous amount of support for artificial intelligence around the world, as it promises new applications and improvements in existing tools. Self-driving cars would rely heavily on AI, as would automated tools that screen MRIs for abnormalities. Each country has a different culture and set of values, which means each will tackle the problem of developing rich AI capabilities with a different mind-set and fervour. Within the context of this book we talk about many startups and other HCM technology companies, many based in the United States simply because the employers that demand advanced human capital technologies are often also based there, offering a target-rich environment for vendors and service providers. However, investment in and further development of AI is a global phenomenon, as this section clearly shows.

China

China is one country that has publicly declared its intent to invest heavily in AI. The country's plan calls for the nation to be the world leader in AI by 2030, which has spurred heavy investments into the company's AI startups and infrastructure. It's entirely possible that China may in fact reach that goal, because the government allows some activities that other countries might not. For instance, public video footage from police cameras in Guangzhou is being provided to facial recognition startups to support data analysis and algorithm development (Horwitz, 2018).[13] We know that the fundamental aspect of being able to create AI tools that are usable and useful is a ready, and large, source of data, and the Chinese government is willing and able to provide that data free of charge. Another step in the pursuit of global AI domination came in an announcement in early 2018. Chinese company Alibaba made headlines when it announced that its AI system was able to beat a human score for the first time in the Stanford University reading and comprehension exam, a test developed by Stanford scientists and based on data available in Wikipedia (Lucas, 2018).[14] The system's neural network was required to crunch the data and respond to more than 100,000 questions. To be fair, Microsoft's own algorithm also beat the human score in this specific competition, but the results took an additional day to compute and finalize, meaning China took the gold in this event.

United Kingdom

The UK is no stranger to AI technologies either. In 2017 many new startups were highlighted in the media as they launched in order to tackle any number of problems, from self-driving vehicles to cybersecurity to background checks. Here are brief examinations of just three of the systems to demonstrate the wide variety of use cases and opportunities to leverage AI in today's fast-paced world of technology development (nanalyze, 2018).[15] For starters, Onfido is a system designed to use facial recognition technology to support identity verification and background screening. Historically this practice has been accomplished by collecting sensitive personal data and can take several days to complete the process, potentially exposing users to identity theft as their data is provided, gathered and submitted. Another tool, BenevolentAI, uses deep learning to mine data from successful drug creation and discovery practices to shorten the time to market for new, potentially life-saving medications. One of the key factors in the high price of medications is the significant lead time and investment in discovery and testing – shortening that period could potentially reduce costs for new medications, making them more accessible to those in need. Finally, OakNorth is an application designed to measure risk. While that would be valuable in any number of industries, it is most beneficial to the financial industry. Leveraging AI, the system would identify and price risks in such a way that firms could make faster, better decisions about credit and lending. In the future, this type of system could augment or even replace actuaries, the individuals that calculate risks and influence prices and offerings in the industry.

Other countries around the world are also racing towards the development and adoption of AI-based technologies, including France, Israel and Canada, to name a few. The takeaway here is that AI technologies are here to stay. The use cases are broad, deep and varied, and there is no way to even begin to predict how much of an impact these smart technologies will have on the way we live and work. The good news is we don't have to know how all of the technology is developed. We don't have to build our own algorithms and systems. We just need to be really clear about the problems we have and the kinds of solutions that can improve the experiences for candidates, employees and business leaders. While the rest of this book might delve into technical bits here or there, for the most part we are done talking about the nuts and bolts of AI technology. Now, let's dive into how AI can apply to the world of HCM.

Additional resources

As promised at the beginning of this chapter, if you are technically minded or interested in diving deeper into the technology components of artificial intelligence, I would recommend exploring the following resources alongside the exhaustive list of reference material I've cited throughout the book. Each of the resources below is full of insightful information from a perspective outside HR, which means you'll spend some energy thinking about how these translate from a broader point of view to the one that matters most to you. Experience has taught me that's a valuable exercise to participate in:

- Stanford One Hundred Year Study on Artificial Intelligence (AI100) – this is a 100-year effort to analyse and examine the potential impacts of AI on the world, including life, work and entertainment.
- *Prediction Machines: The simple economics of artificial intelligence* by Agrawal, Gans and Goldfarb (2018, Harvard Business Review Press) – this book examines the economical side of AI, including how the cheaper cost of predictions has led to more applications and examples of AI being used.

Key points

- AI is the next logical step in business evolution now that we have the capability to capture, store and analyse more data than ever before.
- AI technologies include machine learning, natural language processing and deep learning. Each has use cases that affect our lives in both consumer and workplace contexts.
- Adoption and investment in these technologies is rapidly increasing, and both governments and employers around the world are aggressively pursuing research and development of advanced systems powered by AI.

Notes

1 https://www.bbc.com/news/technology-18419691

2 https://www.bbc.com/news/technology-18475646

3 https://www.sierra-cedar.com/wp-content/uploads/sites/12/2018/01/Sierra-Cedar_2017-2018_HRSystemsSurvey_WhitePaper.pdf

4 https://en.oxforddictionaries.com/definition/artificial_intelligence

5 https://ai100.stanford.edu/2016-report/section-i-what-artificial-intelligence/defining-ai

6 https://link.springer.com/article/10.1007/BF03379600

7 https://medium.com/@katherinebailey/reframing-the-ai-effect-c445f87ea98b

8   http://www.nomodes.com/Larry_Tesler_Consulting/Adages_and_
    Coinages.html

9   https://slator.com/technology/big-tech-using-machine-translation-ai-
    proxy/

10 https://www.nytimes.com/2012/06/26/technology/in-a-big-network-of-
    computers-evidence-of-machine-learning.html

11 https://www.pcworld.com/article/2996620/business/google-reports-
    strong-profit-says-its-rethinking-everything-around-machine-learning.
    html

12 http://files.pitchbook.com/website/files/pdf/PitchBook_1Q_2018_
    Analyst_Note_Real_Potential_for_AI.pdf

13 https://qz.com/1248493/sensetime-the-billion-dollar-alibaba-backed-
    ai-company-thats-quietly-watching-everyone-in-china/

14 https://www.ft.com/content/8763219a-f9bc-11e7-9b32-d7d59aace167

15 https://www.nanalyze.com/2018/05/top-10-british-artificial-
    intelligence-startups-uk/

General AI applications within HCM

If you were tasked with trying to help your workforce understand the potential impacts of AI and robotic process automation on your company, what would be your solution? For Guardian Life, an insurance firm with 11,000 employees and service representatives around the globe, the answer is to schedule a robot play date. Deanna Mulligan is the Chief Executive Officer of Guardian Life, and she knows that in the world of insurance claims, actuarial tables and other components are going to be some of the most easily automated aspects of work. For employees, this can be disconcerting, as they don't know what kind of impact this might have on their jobs. According to Mulligan, she expects only about 10 per cent of the jobs at the firm to be affected by technological advances, but she's not approaching this passively (Kirkland, 2018).[1]

The rest of the firm will be disrupted by the technologies that are coming, and the best way to help the rest of the workforce prepare for that future is to give them opportunities to interact with and understand those technologies – hence the robot play dates. These events allow back-office workers to interact with small robots and take robotics classes to learn more about how the technologies work. More importantly, they see how the robots can improve what they are doing and where the robots can't take over their roles of serving customers. The end goal is to help the workers see that it isn't about workers or AI coming out on top. Instead, it's about finding the best components of both resources and partnering up to better serve the customer base.

I love this example because it shows that we don't have to stick our collective heads in the sand and hope that automation passes us by. In fact, we can embrace it knowing that there are better outcomes ahead. This applies whether you're the CEO at a multinational firm or you're the head of HR for a company with 100 employees. There is tremendous opportunity for automation to bring value into the workplace, and HR is at the forefront of this trend and how it will affect and impact our people. We are strategically positioned to demonstrate for the rest of the business how we leverage these technologies and how they can improve the work environment for all.

AI solves administrative HR problems

One of my favourite quotes from an old friend is that great HR is invisible. If we're doing our jobs correctly, then employees are enjoying their work, getting along with their managers, and performing at their most productive levels. I'd posit that a business has never succeeded wildly and then pointed at consistent and effective HR practices as the key to success, even if that's true. We're focusing instead on the actual results, not the enablers that made it possible.

Similarly, one of the concepts I've found in my research is that when AI works correctly, it's virtually invisible because we're so focused on the end result (not the technology that made it possible). When AI works as it's supposed to, it can be relatively boring. The results might be exciting, but the AI component itself is of little interest once the novelty wears off. That's not necessarily a bad thing, because the priority for us as employers shouldn't be the technology – it should be the outcome. Take self-driving cars, for example. If you've ever ridden in one, the experience is a little bit, well, boring. After the novelty wears off, you lose interest just as you would if you were riding in a taxi or other vehicle where someone else is handling the driving. The reason this poses a challenge is that AI might be seen by some as a fad. Once the novelty wears off, the very concept of AI might be seen as just another 'flash in the pan' instead of the revolutionary technology that it is. I've been very careful in this book to talk about AI not for its flashy 'fun' value, but in the context of the very real problems it solves for you, for me and for businesses around the world. Within this chapter the goal is to introduce you to some of the groundbreaking technologies available today as well as some of the ways they may affect how HR is handled for years to come.

Regardless of the value of the technology, today HR is a highly administrative function. We explored some of the various technological underpinnings in the last chapter and will look at some of the important use cases spanning the full employee lifecycle in forthcoming chapters, but this specific portion of the book is geared toward the administrative components and general applications for AI technologies in the workplace. Some of these might bleed over into other administrative-heavy types of functions like legal or accounting, but because they are an essential part of HR I didn't want to skip over them in my rush to look at recruiting, learning, or talent management.

In the last chapter you saw how much money is flowing into AI technologies from an investment perspective: billions of dollars. And our very own industry is getting its due as well. Last year my friend and colleague George LaRocque of HRWINS tracked a total of US $1 billion-plus in funding rounds spread across 143 separate events in the HR technology industry (LaRocque, 2018).[2] These investments spanned various rounds (seed, A, B, C and beyond), technology focus areas (recruiting, learning, benefits, talent and core HR) and countries (this is a global phenomenon).

In an in-depth analysis of the firms receiving funding, my firm found that nearly half of the investments in HR technology went to firms touting bots, machine learning and other AI features and components (Lighthouse Research, 2018).[3] Based on the volume and the messaging I'm seeing in the industry, I expect this volume to increase into the future, especially in critical automation areas such as sourcing and screening candidates, highlighting employee sentiment and other highly administrative activities. Providers on the list ran the gamut from those focused on data analytics or learning to those exploring the gig economy or employee engagement.

Figure 3.1 depicts a handful of the firms that were categorized as having artificial intelligence technologies in their offerings.

Figure 3.1   AI-focused HR technology firms receiving 2017 venture capital funding

Talent acquisition	Learning and development
• Lever – Applicant Tracking • WorkMarket – Contingent Worker Mgt • Textio – Augmented Writing • Shiftig – Contingent Worker Mgt • Entelo – Candidate Sourcing	• Grovo – Microlearning • Butterfly – Manager Coaching • Blue Canoe – Language Learning • Sunlight – Employee Development Bot

Talent management	Core HR and workforce
• CultureAmp – Surveys and Feedback • Glint – Surveys and Feedback • Energage – Surveys and Feedback • Rally Team – Internal Mobility • Ascendify – Internal Mobility Bot	• Lumity – Employee Benefits • Visier – Predictive Analytics • Legion – Workforce Scheduling • Spoke – Employee Service Chatbot

SOURCE 2017 Lighthouse Research & Advisory

To provide some context, these are five examples of firms that received funding:

- Butterfly received $2.4 million for its AI-driven coaching insights tool. Every manager needs help, but companies can't offer a tailored approach for every manager. Butterfly overcomes this issue by offering intelligent insights for managers based on anonymous employee survey results and past performance data, then offers coaching insights or recommended training to fill gaps.

- Lumity picked up $14 million to support its benefits management platform. Focusing on SMB issues around benefits administration, the system's machine learning algorithms offer insights and customized benefit recommendations to help support a range of employee needs.

- onQ, a group communication and learning platform, scooped up $7 million to improve its system. One of the biggest priorities for onQ is leveraging machine learning models to score learner engagement, influence, sentiment, facilitation and other outcomes. Instead of looking just at completion rates or assessment scores, companies can now actually understand whether learners are truly engaged in their learning experiences.

- Spoke, founded by three Google alumni, was funded to the tune of $28 million for its employee self-service chatbot. In Spoke's research, it has found that nearly half of requests to HR departments can be answered immediately based on available information, which frees up HR teams to focus on higher-priority items. This bot serves as a point of contact for employees and pricing is based on usage, not a set employee headcount.

- Ascendify, a talent acquisition and management platform that focuses on enterprise firms, received $11 million in funding. The company just unveiled its new Aspire product, an automated bot that supports employees looking for internal mobility opportunities by helping them understand what skills they already have, what skills they need and the delta between their current and future planned role(s).

As new funding rounds continue to occur, I expect to see additional money poured into firms that are leveraging AI technologies like machine learning and natural language processing to help automate tasks, speed up solution delivery and personalize service for workers. There is incredible value in these types of technology to change the workplace landscape for the better.

What about the impact on jobs?

Virtually every AI-related discussion I've had with executives and technology providers in the last few years has revolved around a central question: what will AI do to our jobs? For instance, a 2016 Pew survey showed that about two-thirds of respondents expected robots to do much of the work of humans in approximately 50 years;

however, four out of five of those same respondents said, 'But not *my* job' (Abbruzzese).[4] Did you catch the maths paradox there? Sixty-seven per cent of people think jobs will change but 80 per cent say it won't change their own job. It's a classic example of overvaluing the skills we have and undervaluing the skills of others in an attempt to save face, and I've pointed at this research in numerous presentations to help show that we can be incredibly irrational when faced with fears of job loss or irrelevance. Don't worry, I don't follow that logic. Not only am I a technological optimist, I'm also a pragmatist. Every time technology changes to the degree it starts impacting jobs, new jobs are created. While news items like the Pew research survey make for interesting headlines, in reality there's no way for the general public to know how much of an impact robots, algorithms and AI will have in the next five years, much less 50 years into the future. To take a step back and look at the question objectively, this kind of technological advancement has happened literally thousands of times throughout history, from the earliest plough to the invention of the personal computer. New technologies are created that disrupt and change how an industry operates, and the people that are displaced must find new roles and opportunities for employment.

One example of this concept is search engines. Around the world, millions of searches per day are leading people to articles, videos, social sites and other online resources. How do they find what they are looking for? *Search engines*. In order to help websites improve rankings and be seen by more people, companies employ specialists in SEO, or search engine optimization. Think about it: even as recently as 1990, search engine optimization did not exist. Nobody held a job as an SEO expert within an agency, as a freelancer, or as a consultant. Today, a quick search of a popular global job board shows more than 3,000 job listings for individuals with search engine optimization expertise, and a search on LinkedIn shows more than 500,000 professionals with some variation of 'search engine optimization' in their job title or skills. The parallel is clear: even as mature industries are disrupted, new industries and opportunities are born.

There's definite optimism within the ranks of the HR profession about the value AI can bring. A 2017 study by the Canadian HR Professionals Association (HRPA) found that 84 per cent of HR professionals felt that AI was a valuable tool for supporting human resources objectives, yet most HR leaders are not yet very familiar with how AI operates and the type of value it can provide.[5] This was echoed in a study my team performed. While recruiting is the primary area of development for most AI tools today, a survey of recruiting leaders put AI dead last in terms of priorities for 2017 (Lighthouse Research, 2017).[6] Is this because artificial intelligence doesn't have value or isn't going to improve the profession? Certainly not! It's more likely that the audience didn't have a good frame of reference for how AI works and the particular use cases that matter to them, which may have shifted the rankings considerably.

Despite these positive beliefs, many of the initial conversations about AI turn to how the adoption of these technologies will impact jobs globally, not just within the HR profession. Whether for the shock value or some other reason, it's hard to enter a discussion that doesn't have this job loss component as one of the key storylines. However, for the purposes of this conversation, we are going to focus more keenly on the actual jobs of HR professionals in an attempt to understand the degree to which this automation and/or replacement may happen. Taking a more specific look at human resources, it's easy to see ways that the advance of AI could disrupt how businesses have operated for quite some time. Human resources as a profession is relatively young, but it is still heavily administrative in most companies.

From setting up employee taxes and benefits during the early days of onboarding to sifting through hundreds of resumes a year for job openings, the administrative, hands-on work of human resources is ripe for disruption and automation. For instance, one recent client my team supported during an HR technology selection was using nearly 50 per cent of the HR team's time to do duplicate work. Time was tracked in a specific system, but the HR team then had to analyse the time and fill any gaps by hand. Then, the team would manually enter any vacation or sick leave into the system to ensure everyone had the correct number of hours on their time sheet. After that, the data was downloaded and then uploaded into the payroll processing tool. That data from payroll, however, never made it back into the main system of record. It stayed separate and siloed, and it could never be reported on in a holistic fashion alongside any other pertinent HR data. This example shows ample opportunities for robotic process automation. This story is incredibly common, which is why the 2018 research study by Leapgen showed that half of employers are currently or planning to implement automation into routine tasks (Brennan).[7]

The concept of 'swivel chair automation', or an algorithm designed to pull data from one system and insert it into another, has a clear linkage to the types of work done in many HR organizations. Another tangible example of this comes to us from a provider of automated chatbot tools for recruiting purposes. One client of the company was a large cosmetics firm looking to hire a series of brand ambassadors with large social media followings in order to capitalize on the reach and influence those people would offer. In the actual chat interactions with candidates on the website, the algorithm would ask the person about their most active social media channel and username, and then it would automatically go and pull in their data in the background, storing it with their application. For example, if the person said that Twitter was their preferred channel, the system could automatically check the person's Twitter handle and their number of followers and interactions in recent history. Someone with 10,000 engaged followers would be much more appealing as a candidate than someone with 20 passive followers. This would be challenging and time-consuming to handle as a physical human task, but the chatbot algorithm accomplishes this virtually instantaneously.

Human interaction, non-human systems

One reality of adopting artificial intelligence is that workers, including HR, will have to work alongside systems and processes that are automated. How does this affect us? To what degree are we prepared for this sort of work environment? During a briefing with the team that runs Paradox.ai, a bot designed to support recruiting and candidate engagement, one of the company's representatives unveiled a surprising statistic. Candidates typically know they are chatting with a computer system called 'Olivia' during the application process, but at the end of the conversation, approximately 75 per cent of candidates actually thank the bot for the interaction. It's hard to know how much of this is simple routine, but the fact remains that we will have to understand how the relationship operates and to what degree we should humanize the algorithms that interact with candidates and employees within these systems.

To make this point about how humans can interact with non-human systems, let's look at one of the biggest pain points for workers everywhere: scheduling meetings. One of the common tools in use today by busy business professionals is a scheduling application to manage their calendars and appointments. To avoid the back-and-forth hassle created by attempting to schedule meetings via seemingly endless volleys of e-mail, these scheduling apps let users synchronize calendars and then share that calendar with people they want to meet with, making the process more passive and automated. There are a variety of tools offering this functionality, but one that stood out in the research was Zoom.ai. Zoom.ai is positioned as an automated assistant available to support the needs of the workforce in a variety of needs beyond the common scheduling application. For instance, while many of us scramble to pull together notes or information about who we are meeting with, Zoom.ai will actually gather that social data and provide it automatically prior to the meeting. Other uses include document generation, transcribing phone calls and more. The way this technology operates is simple: users leverage their favourite messaging platform to interact with the system, submitting requests that are then managed and handled by the algorithm. Messaging platforms can be anything from Microsoft Teams and Slack to Facebook Messenger, Skype, or even SMS text messages.

In the end, for many workers it comes down to productivity. Can AI help us to be more productive? One research study estimated the cost of lost productivity due to non-job-related administrative work at $4,600 *per employee* (Gorman, 2017).[8] Imagine for a second that you run a company with 1,000 employees. On average, workers at your firm would be wasting $4.6 million on those kinds of tasks that might not even add that much value to the business. The more we can give these tasks to AI, the more we can turn our employees toward things that impact the business. Things that drive value for customers. Things that *matter*.

Types of broad-spectrum AI components in HCM

In the last chapter we covered some of the basics of how machine learning and natural language processing work. Now we can begin to analyse types of broad-spectrum AI components that can be leveraged within the human capital management function. While these continue to develop every day, at the time of writing there are already dozens of systems focused on a variety of HR tasks being automated and augmented with AI. Remember, the tasks to prioritize with automation are those that are high volume and repetitive. The more specialized a specific task might be, the better. Some tasks are urgent – they need to get done quickly. Other tasks are important – their completion has a critical impact. If you think about this as a four-quadrant grid mapped to urgency and importance (Table 3.1) this allows someone to complete more work than ever before in those areas that are important but not urgent or urgent but not important.

Historically, an individual might have delegated a task that was urgent but not important, such as scheduling meetings or gathering employment contract data, to a person. Today, automated systems can easily accomplish these and other similar tasks with a chatbot. Within a few seconds the system can handle what previously took anywhere from a few minutes up to half an hour, depending on how systems are organized and documents are stored. Similarly, while items in the lower-right quadrant might have been completely ignored or overlooked in the past, it's possible that some of those actions are now able to be handled by a computer. For instance, reading through every piece of employee feedback and synthesizing a few key points and themes from the content would not have been a task most

Table 3.1 Task prioritization matrix

	Urgent	Not urgent
Important	Do	Plan
Not Important	Delegate	Eliminate

employers would be willing to pay a worker to do, especially if the firm has thousands of workers. Yet systems such as the ones highlighted below can do this rapidly in near real time. There are literally hundreds of uses spanning almost any task that an HR leader might have to accomplish, so let's explore some of the more pertinent ones that have advanced pretty quickly in terms of development.

Employee sentiment analysis

Language is the fundamental currency for how people express themselves. The concept behind sentiment analysis is pretty simple: analyse large amounts of text and categorize them by sentiment or attitude. The value is clear. By understanding the general mood for a population of employees, whether globally, by department, or location, a company can better serve those workers and meet their needs. This is done by blending natural language processing with machine learning. Sentiment analysis relies on open, unstructured text from conversations, e-mails and other qualitative inputs. Additionally, machine learning is used to train the system on words to look for that might signify issues. If all workers in a specific function mention salary or working hours in their communications or survey responses, then the systems can flag those areas for review by an HR representative.

One example of a sentiment analysis platform is provided by technology startup Tigli Solutions. The tool analyses e-mail data to determine engagement, leadership, alignment and other elements. It's common for systems to look at engagement as a factor, but because Tigli plugs into the e-mail server data, it can look more specifically at who is e-mailing whom, whether they are having personal or work-focused conversations, and more. While the system is anonymous and does not identify users directly, it can derive sentiments down to the departmental level, giving employers the opportunity to address issues and hot spots before they become a major problem.

Ultimate Software's Xander AI is similar in its approach. The firm is doing its best to blend analytical intelligence with emotional intelligence to get a fully accurate picture of what is going on in the organization. The analysis then powers predictions, custom recommendations and more. Instead of focusing on e-mail data, Xander picks up other qualitative inputs from performance review comments, social commentary on the company intranet and employee survey feedback. The machine learning has been trained to the point where it can understand general sentiment by extrapolating the user's mood from the text. For example, if someone types, 'The internet connection is too slow at the office', the system intuitively knows this is a negative issue. Alternatively, if someone types, 'I have a great team', the system will associate this with positive feelings. While it is easy to look at these examples and understand the intent from a human perspective, it's not as easy for machines to navigate the nuances of language, and that doesn't even involve the effort and challenge required for performing this analysis tens of thousands of times.

A final example comes from employee feedback platform Culture Amp. A certified B Corporation, the Melbourne-based software provider's goal is to help employers capture and act on employee feedback. Head of Industry and Public Relations for Culture Amp, Damon Klotz, told me, 'Many companies have traditionally given employees the *illusion of listening*. Instead of really listening to what needed to be done and then fixing it, they would collect survey data and then sit on it, often letting the problems go unchecked over time.' For the last few years since its inception, the company has focused very heavily on the survey design and feedback collection processes. It now has a text analysis tool that offers employers insights into employee sentiment. Unlike some text analysis tools that are trained using a wide variety of unstructured data sets, Culture Amp feels like its tool is better suited for employer purposes because the machine learning algorithms were developed using thousands of employee feedback comments gathered during the first few years of the company's existence.

Verbal communication and interaction

While e-mail is one of the most commonly used tools for workplace communication, there's no substitute for stepping into someone's office for a quick conversation. Verbal communication always has been and will continue to be a quick way to interact, and now the second party in that interaction can be a machine, not just a person. Virtually all of us have used a voice-based app on our devices to help us with searches, directions, or other tasks – Apple's Siri, Amazon's Alexa, Microsoft's Cortana and Google's assistant all fill this need.

What's more, voice interactivity has a variety of points that add to the value the system can bring. For instance, most people can speak faster than they can type. Additionally, those with mobility issues or impairments might not be able to use a standard keyboard, but voice interaction might offer them a way to interact with devices in a seamless manner. It also could increase safety if someone can focus on a task while speaking to a system without having to look at a screen to type out a message. These are some of the reasons we have all become enamoured with our various mobile assistants on our smartphones, and there's no reason to believe this technology can't also add value to the HR environment.

'How much vacation time do I have?' In a demonstration at the company's annual user conference, Infor's product team showed off its voice capabilities and highlighted some of the coming improvements in the system functionality. While examples like the vacation balance request above require a user to initiate contact, other opportunities for voice interactivity can take two paths: proactive responses and proactive initiation. For instance, a proactive response to the question above might be, 'You have 65 hours of vacation. Would you like to schedule some time off?' On the other hand, a proactive initiation might be a notification from the system based on an analysis of vacation balances across the organization compared to the individual's balance, a policy capping vacation hours, or something else highly tailored. For example, 'Alex, I noticed you have accrued 118 hours of vacation. Our policy limits accruals to 120 hours, which means you will not receive any additional hours for the coming pay periods unless you take some time off. Would you like to schedule this now?' In each instance, it's almost as if the employee has a coach guiding them through the conversation, yet it's nothing more than a voice-interactive algorithm programmed to interact based on preset criteria or parameters.

One of the interesting opportunities for incorporating devices like smart speakers into the workplace is having them listen in on conversations and then provide insights after the fact. What if your speaker could listen in on the calls your sales team makes and then give them ideas on how to improve their results? Alternatively, what if your speaker could listen to managers and then give them tips and ideas on how to improve their coaching and feedback style? There are questions, and there should be, about what might be recorded and how that information would be used, but it's a great example of the future prospects of what these types of technologies can offer in terms of performance support. I have yet to see a technology in the market that is this advanced, but I know that we're getting closer to these types of advancements in proactive technologies to help us all manage our workloads, and our performance, more effectively.

CASE STUDY   Wearables: mechanizing human networking and relationships

You've been invited to a networking meeting in your company, but you really don't want to go. After all, every time you attend one of these things you end up standing by yourself in the corner checking out the latest buzz on your social media feeds on your smartphone. But this time it's different. You're wearing a badge that will light up when you get near someone with similar interests. As you walk through the group navigating your way to the refreshments, you see your initials pop up on someone's badge nearby and you stop to greet them. After a moment or two you realize you both have previous experience working for the same company in a different industry. You spend some time getting to know this person and then continue on your journey to get a drink, promising yourself you'll reach out when you're back in the office because the individual's area of expertise is one your team needs for an upcoming project. As you arrive at the table, your badge lights up with someone else's initials, and you turn around to greet them. You quickly realize that while your backgrounds are different, you have a connection in your mutual love for children's charities. That starts the conversation, but before long you're discussing work projects and how you have overcome similar challenges in your respective roles. It's not even 10 minutes into the event and you've already made two new connections you didn't have before.

This story is one of the first examples I've seen of HR technology hardware making its way into the employee experience by way of a wearable. We're used to software doing much of the work, and there's definitely a software component in this vendor's solution, but the hardware element in the form of a wearable device is intriguing because it is primarily a visual cueing system powered by a software matching algorithm. This system was developed by Chicago-based Proxfinity, and it works by having users answer a set of questions prior to an event. Those questions could have a variety of designs, from looking for ways to connect people with similar interests (as in the example above) or looking for ways to connect people from teams and departments across the organization to break down silos and improve communications.

What impressed me in particular was the analytics dashboard that employers can review after an event. For example, if the system was used for an employee onboarding event to help make sure executives socialize with new hires, the team can analyse the reports after the fact to see if the executive team hung out together during the event or if they were truly dispersed into the crowd and making connections with the new hires. While this system isn't yet AI-powered, it's a short step to incorporate some level of machine learning to support these interactions. One component in a future artificially intelligent algorithm might be helping to connect diverse individuals with key leaders, putting people together without the benefit of the survey (using data from their employee profile, performance goals, and so on), or even matching high-performing individuals with each other to spur innovation and idea generation.

As of today there are not many wearable use cases within the HR technology realm beyond things like activity trackers that help with wellness initiatives. The advent of more smart technologies will open up the opportunity for AI to make its way into the hardware side of the equation, which offers an entirely different layer of information for algorithms to factor into their calculations. When you think about it, today algorithms are half-blind to the activities that occur in the workplace. Sentiment analysis systems can see our virtual and electronic traffic and activities, but our physical interactions are outside the scope of the system for the most part. Creating this layer of data will enable artificially intelligent systems to look for even better ways to help us improve the results we see with our human capital.

Automated chatbots

Bots. We've profiled a few of them already (and have several more to go before we're finished). It seems we can't turn around today without being inundated by yet another chatbot that fills a communication gap in some form or fashion. That's because they work, they are inexpensive compared to human labour, and they can be programmed to fit a company's verbal preferences, giving it a personalized feel. Interestingly, one common complaint in some industry circles is that chatbots should not be included in AI discussions because they are typically nothing more than a library of responses that are used to respond to conversational comments. Those detractors say that the systems lack the machine learning components that get smarter with every human interaction. However, they are still automating key parts of the business and its talent processes, which means that for our purposes they are worth exploring.

One point of value for chatbots is the opportunity for employers to customize the language and wording so that the interactive assistant mirrors the culture of the firm. For instance, an employer with a strong focus on customer service might have the bot responses programmed to use more language focusing on customer service or in screening questions dedicated to that topic. Alternatively, if the company is interested in being seen as having a creative or 'fun' culture, it can plan for the bot to crack jokes, build rapport and share glimpses of the culture through the various interactions with candidates and employees.

Another example of chatbots supporting HR practices? Gifts. Recently I had the opportunity to try out Eva, a bot that sends out gifts to users, clients and candidates. From an HR perspective, it could easily be used to send candidates a 'thank you' for their time, but it could also be used for employees that need a special recognition for a job well done. The bot interacts with users via a simple chat interface, quizzing them on their likes, dislikes and preferences. For instance, during the conversation I mentioned I don't drink, so Eva didn't send me a bottle of wine. Instead, the application sent me a sampling of dark chocolate because my tastes tend to lean toward the sweet side.

On a more serious note, one area where I believe bots can help employers in an incredible way is by increasing HCM software adoption rates. While it seems like a 'meta' discussion, it might be one of the *most undervalued* points when it comes to bots supporting HR's needs. Why do adoption rates matter? Well, for those of us that focus our efforts on analysing HR technology, we find that one of the top reasons people select technology is because of usability. Essentially, if a piece of software is intuitive and easy to use, it will be more valuable to the organization. Bots help to make that interaction more seamless: it's easier to utilize a chat conversation than to try to find a help manual or knowledgebase to learn how to use a piece of technology.

Think about it this way: when a vendor sells a product to a buyer, the value promise is based on full adoption of the system. For instance, adoption of a recognition tool might promise up to 10 per cent reductions in regrettable employee turnover or a substantial increase in employee engagement scores. However, if half the employees or managers refuse to use the tool, there's no way it can meet the needs of the business or generate the anticipated ROI. It's like trying to create a new process to save resources and having half the employees use the old process, negating the value of the process change.

In instances where a firm has integrated bots into the product, such as RamcoHCM, this can lead to higher adoption rates. This is credited in large part to the technology's chatbots that are present on Skype, Slack, Facebook Messenger, e-mail and even text messaging. Employees can interact with the HR system via any of these channels according to the employee's own preference. For instance, if workers prefer e-mail, they can use Ramco's e-mail tools to handle HR-related tasks. If SMS is the preferred communication tool, employees can get pay slips and do chat-based interactions even on basic phones. While smartphones are fairly ubiquitous, there are still areas of the world and portions of the population where they are not fully utilized. Even workers with 'dumb' phones that only have basic texting capabilities (no internet access) can use these SMS-based tools to get work done.

Additionally, automation can be used to help users learn how to use new software. WalkMe is a provider of technology that helps businesses ease onboarding with new technology solutions. The system uses a combination of AI and analytics to predict user behaviours and offer step-by-step assistance to increase engagement and uptake with new systems. I constantly hear about the 'user experience' from technology providers and how they are trying to create a positive one, and this example of having an assistant or tool to guide you through the process as a new user of a system is a great example of how to create an experience that users won't soon forget.

At this point we're seeing more and more uses for bots in almost any area of HR that is heavily administrative or routine. We will delve into other uses for bots in future chapters, as they are being heavily adopted and leveraged in the talent acquisition process for candidate engagement and screening. They are also being leveraged to support employee engagement and recognition, an area where HR often coaches managers. That sort of coaching practice can slip through the cracks of a busy workload for many HR leaders, which is why bots make the perfect assistant for those types of instances.

Facial recognition tools

In the last chapter I talked about the challenges of creating facial recognition systems. As humans we can quickly scan and sort faces to learn who is who, but algorithms have a harder time mapping the contours of the face, creating unique maps of each individual person, and accounting for hats, scarves, glasses, or other obscuring items. Additionally, we always assume that facial recognition works because it has a clear frontal photograph to work with. In reality, photos can capture either side of a face or someone looking away from the camera, which sometimes makes identification challenging even to the human eye.

Despite the challenges, several photo storage and sharing tools today have the ability to recognize faces from a variety of photos automatically, and this sort of advancement is also relevant to the workplace. In a discussion with one firm in the HCM technology industry, the representative showed me the company's innovative employee check-in system. This company uses a simple wall-mounted tablet with facial recognition software in the front office of the building to capture your time of check-in and check-out for payroll purposes. When an employee walks in, it quickly scans the person's face and projects a short welcome message on the wall monitor. This helps not only with check-in time, logging their attendance records, but with security and safety as well.

Facial recognition will get more visibility as a topic in the chapter on talent acquisition, because video hiring and interviewing solutions are making increasing use of algorithms to process video content and understand if the interviewee is looking at the camera or reading a script off-screen. By looking at the position of the eye and the direction it's looking, the system can flag a person if it seems like they are potentially cheating.

The future? Forecasting HR advancements based on current technology

Retail workers will be able to point their mobile device's camera at a specific area of the clothing display and the system will recognize the product, offering up a variety of helpful information to support the associate in real time. The device will bring up sales history for that item, including graphical representations of pricing data over time. It will also display forecasted sales based on current purchasing trends. In addition, the system can use that predicted sales forecast to suggest sales discounts or pricing strategies to maximize revenue.

While this sounds fantastical, it isn't science fiction. It's one of many capabilities of Coleman, the AI tool that powers Infor's systems across a variety of industry verticals and its HCM platform. Infor is a multinational enterprise software company headquartered in New York City. The AI system is named for Katherine Coleman Johnson, a physicist and mathematician whose brainpower and willpower helped man reach the moon in the 1960s, and it is embedded throughout Infor's suite of products, from healthcare and retail to human capital and supply chain management.

While this technology is amazing, the use case is focused on retail; however, it's easy to translate this visual recognition capability into the HCM spectrum. For instance, what if a computer can recognize an employee's face in order to log them into an attendance tracking system? Or maybe it analyses a person and determines the best training modality for a particular employee's learning style based on previous training and performance? It might even suggest potential career paths by factoring in the skills, training and aspirations of the worker.

While not all of these capabilities currently exist *together*, almost all of them are out-of-the-box features for a variety of best-of-breed technology vendors in the human capital management technology industry. It's exciting to think about how these advances, taken as a whole, might shift how companies perceive, manage and engage with the workforce.

Understanding and quantifying the value of AI systems

Despite the inherent excitement that comes from the capabilities these systems offer, it's important as a business leader to understand the value of AI-based technologies. Is it more flash than substance? Do they really do all the things they claim, and if so, what value does that add to the business? Throughout this book, discussions will turn to various value points, but let's look at some areas where potential value lies:

1 **Productivity.** According to Zoom.ai's research, the most active users leveraging the company's automated assistant typically save up to 25 hours a month, averaging more than $16,000 saved for an employee with a $100,000 salary. Now, scale that across hundreds or thousands of corporate users, and it's easy to see how this becomes an incredible value proposition for the power of AI.

2 **Adoption rates.** It's harder to pin a value on this, yet that doesn't mean it's any less important. As covered in the section above focusing on chatbots, the idea that employees, managers and executives would be more connected with and enabled by their firm's technology is a powerful one.

3 **Performance of HR.** Can we get more things accomplished if the 'grunt work' is being handled by algorithms and software? In Table 3.1 earlier in this chapter you saw the diverse classifications for tasks: how many non-urgent or non-important tasks might be

captured and managed by AI technologies, freeing up HR leaders to focus on the more urgent and/or important activities?

4 Retention. While listing any specific number would be subjective, the truth is that AI tools help with hiring practices, which could lead to better employee fit and longer tenures. Additionally, the tools supporting development and employee growth would naturally increase satisfaction, adding yet another layer of possibility to the retention figure. It's too early to attribute a hard figure to this, but it is logical to assume there is a connection.

One final note on value: HR is a profession that, in general, seems to have challenges proving the value it can bring, and the investments in HR technology (whether inclusive of AI or not) also face those same challenges. That's not necessarily a bad thing – we all need to be able to prove what we bring to the table as business leaders. However, what's interesting is that executives clearly see the value HR technology can bring. In one 2017 research study, we found that more business executives *outside* HR thought their HR systems were strategic tools than the executives working *within* HR (Lighthouse Research).[9] This is counterintuitive, but it's also heartening to know that there is already a measure of support for HR technology investment throughout the C-suite. The conversation about the business value of HR technology doesn't stop there, but it's certainly a good place to start.

Key points

- Investment into companies that develop AI-enabled HR software has reached an all-time high and will most likely continue to climb.

- Jobs may or may not be impacted by artificial intelligence, but what we do know is that there are incredibly valuable use cases spanning everything from hiring and training to engagement and beyond.

- Verbal interaction, chatbots and facial recognition software offer just a few of the foundational components of artificial intelligence technology that feed up into the complex uses that span the HCM spectrum.

Notes

1 https://www.mckinsey.com/business-functions/organization/our-insights/the-ceo-of-guardian-life-on-talent-in-an-age-of-digital-disruption

2 http://larocqueinc.com/2017-hr-tech-vc-look-back/

3 http://lhra.io/blog/nearly-half-2017-hr-tech-funding-events-ai-focused-companies/

4 https://mashable.com/2016/03/10/robots-are-coming-to-take-our-jobs-just-not-my-job/#jvmDzzeHWuqF

5 https://www.hrpa.ca/Documents/Public/Thought-Leadership/HRPA-Report-Artificial-Intelligence-20171031.PDF

6 http://lhra.io/blog/2017-talent-acquisition-priorities/

7 https://medium.com/shape-the-future/results-are-in-investments-in-digital-hr-technology-are-fast-becoming-a-reality-but-innovation-4222c0aa9b99

8 https://www.tlnt.com/guess-who-wastes-time-at-work/

9 http://lhra.io/blog/business-value-hr-technology-research-preview/

Core HR and workforce management

04

The client looked at me hopefully after explaining her company's current predicament. While still a fairly small company of just under 300 staff members, the complexities of managing time, attendance and payroll were more than the HR team (a deeply passionate staff of one) could handle. We were in the early planning stages of a technology selection and it was very apparent what this firm needed: automation. Trying to juggle multiple systems, one of which was hosted locally and faced regular downtime issues, was more than she could bear. Every time the time tracking system went down she had to get out the paper sheets and manually sort through timecards to understand who worked on what project and when. In addition, every data entry task she completed was duplicated amongst several systems. And when she finally finished all the reconciliations for time, attendance and leave, it was time to export the data, upload into the payroll system, and start the process all over again for the next pay period.

On the other end of the spectrum, just a few days before I had been talking with a 3,000-employee firm trying to move away from in-house systems built by the company's IT staff. What worked as a homegrown system for 500 employees just didn't scale up to thousands of employees, and that led to a growing set of challenges and frustrations. For instance, there was no official system of record. Payroll had a system. Time and attendance tracking was totally separate. Performance, learning and recruiting all had their own systems. At any one time, getting something as simple as a headcount figure was virtually impossible. Querying the respective systems would return a variety of answers, each of them 'correct' in their own way. Our goal was to consolidate and craft a plan for aligning the new, integrated system with the firm's growth plans and culture.

Both of these stories are not only true – they represent a wide swathe of employers around the world. HR technology can be problematic because companies either buy targeted point solutions as they grow, outpacing the capabilities they need to keep the firm operational, or they buy a large, complex system that sacrifices some capabilities and features for integration and data integrity. In the coming chapters we will look at the technology solutions that meet a specific set of needs at virtually every company, but for now we'll look at the core HR component because it's the most relevant to the largest audience. After all, who doesn't have to track who works and pay those employees for their time?

Workforce management, payroll and risk management are some of the fundamental, core functions of human resources. While they may not be the most glamorous items on the 'to do' list for HR leaders, these and other practices form the fundamental underpinnings of a great function. Not sure if that's true? Try letting payroll slip by a few days and see what happens. Or the next time something pops up that has compliance impacts, why not just let it slide for a few weeks and watch the ramifications. Seriously, though, the need for companies to deliver on these fundamental HR service offerings is critical to business continuity. With the advent of artificial intelligence applications into some of the fundamental aspects of how HR operates, companies now have additional capabilities to support their needs.

While it's somewhat vague, this concept of 'core HR' is going to focus on a handful of specific aspects of the human resources function that don't easily sit in other buckets, such as talent management, learning and development, or talent acquisition. For instance, we will examine how AI affects workforce management applications such as scheduling shifts for workers. In addition, we will explore benefits administration and the technologies that are simplifying that process for employers. The conversation will also include compliance and discrimination, a hot topic in the workplace made even hotter by public firings for harassing behaviours in recent history.

Workforce management

Who's scheduled to work tomorrow? What if I told you that there are systems with the capability to not only help with the transactional aspects of scheduling workers for upcoming shifts, but that the system could also predict the optimal scheduling mix of employees to deliver the most value to the business and its customers? This is a reality in the healthcare field with Infor's Care Workloads product. The tool is designed to understand the competencies of specific nurses and align them with patient needs as the schedule is being built, giving the patients access to the right caregivers at the right time. Similarly, by matching up patients with the unique competencies of a particular nurse, that practitioner will feel validated. Everyone wants to know that their skills are valued and important, and this type of workforce management tool helps to do that for these workers.

The practical impact of expanding this 'smart scheduling' capability into other areas is pretty astounding. For example, what if you could predict in your retail stores which team members work best together to create the best customer experience, increasing sales? Instead of looking at scheduling as a transactional action, employers would think more strategically about how to combine different skills, personalities and competencies to create the right team for the right challenge. Maybe one group is better suited for those intensely busy times with high volume and high stress, while another group is better suited to the slower times because they can engage with customers more deeply or develop creative merchandise displays that customers love. This area will continue to mature as companies have the opportunity to connect more information sources like sales volume with their workforce management and scheduling data.

While we're exploring fundamentals of workforce management, swapping shifts is one of those activities that can be challenging, painful, annoying, or a combination of all three. Any worker that's traded shifts in the past knows that it can be difficult to find the right person, contact them, and make the change in the requisite system. At its 2017 user conference, Ceridian demonstrated its Amazon Alexa voice interactivity capabilities, one of which helps to solve this problem handily.[1] In the demonstration of Dayforce Voice, an employee goes through a short interactive dialogue to swap a shift with a particular colleague and even schedule time away from work. While those processes are not new or noteworthy, the idea of employees being able to accomplish those tasks with a voice interface is very impressive.

Another firm working to manage the administrative needs of scheduling and workforce management is Kronos. One use case is around employees swapping shifts. In the past, basic logic and rules governed the process for who you could swap a shift with. However, the system is attempting to speed up the process by highlighting the people you typically swap with over a period of time and making smart recommendations based on those actions. The algorithm essentially learns your behaviours, knows who is most likely to accept that particular shift on that particular day, and then it targets them with the request. Managers also get an upgraded experience with visual tools that automatically highlight which shift requests are okay to grant and which need human intervention, potentially saving the manager time in navigating multiple employee schedules. The platform boasts an automated chatbot that interacts with employees to support interactive time off requests and can automatically notify managers if dates are open. The bot doesn't replace the process – it helps to speed it up by having the schedules and shifts all in one place and giving workers and managers an assistant to facilitate the conversation. Because the chatbot is natively integrated with Microsoft Teams, one of the most common enterprise collaboration tools, and doesn't require a separate interface, users can more easily access the tool. In most cases, user adoption of new technologies increases when vendors can find a way to get the interactive component into the flow of work, such as embedding it within an already-used chat tool or putting links into the company's intranet for easy access.

While time tracking and attendance can seem like a mundane concept in the bigger picture of HCM, the team at Replicon sees it as anything but. In a conversation with some of the key executives at the workforce management technology firm, they explained the firm's vision of 'time intelligence', or giving employers granular insights into how the time is spent by their employees.[2] For example, in a

200-person firm, business leaders have about 400,000 total work hours a year to track and manage. While the business probably has highly detailed accounting records of what money was spent on its expenses, it's probably less clear about how that aggregate set of hours connects to actual objectives and outcomes. That happens partly by being very clear about accuracy on the time tracking side of the equation. One example of the firm's innovative approach is in its facial recognition time clocks. Workers simply walk up to the interface briefly and the platform clocks them in for their shift. There are no buttons or physical interactions required, and as a bonus, there's no way for other workers to 'buddy punch', the practice of clocking in a friend before they arrive so they get full credit for the shift.

Payroll

After workers have been scheduled and employees have completed their shifts, it's time to make sure everyone gets paid. Employers today have a variety of choices for running payroll, and in spite of the powerful and relatively inexpensive options in the market, many firms still use homegrown solutions to run payroll. However, according to some new research, this can be more costly than previously imagined. Homegrown payroll systems have an error rate averaging just over 11 per cent, but employers using a third-party technology or service see error rates around 6 per cent (Lombardi, 2018).[3] The cost of payroll errors isn't just the time to correct the issue. You also need to factor in the very real discussions the affected employee will have with their peers in the workplace, potentially harming engagement and performance.

Anyone that has run payroll knows that the actual process itself is ripe for disruption by AI; a highly repetitive, specialized process must be run on a regular schedule with data that is significantly the same over multiple periods of time. Oh, and let's not forget the incredibly high cost of errors within the payroll process. Forget about getting the most productivity out of an employee with an incorrect pay slip – you'll be lucky to keep them engaged at all. At the same time, any HR leader with a measure of credibility would hesitate to turn over the payroll process to an algorithm. This unveils a critical decision point that is going to increasingly become a common discussion in firms as AI continues its advance: where do we turn over control to a computer and where do we retain it?

In this specific instance, it's probably best to have AI process the initial steps and have a human review the final version prior to submission. This has several benefits. First, the most repetitive, time-consuming aspects of running payroll come in the initial entries and checks. Are all hours accounted for? Have employees used the correct codes? Is overtime being calculated for the correct workers? What about shift differentials and other pay modifications? And so on. The initial steps of processing payroll are fairly routine and can include a variety of these types of questions. Then, after that has been completed and a draft payroll has been run, the payroll administrator is best suited to the task of reviewing the data for completeness and accuracy.

While this isn't foolproof, it does bring to bear the best that humans and software algorithms have to offer. A human can easily see if a common deduction is incorrectly calculated or if a person on leave is being paid accurately for their time off. At the same time, the algorithm powering the payroll engine can do all kinds of instant calculations that a human wouldn't be suited for, such as determining payroll tax rates for individual regions, cities and localities. For instance, at one former employer our team was flummoxed by a pair of employees living across the street from each other that seemingly owed different types of payroll taxes. An algorithm using employee residential data combined with a tax rules engine would quickly be able to sort individuals into their proper municipalities and calculate respective tax rates on the fly.

One reason pay and compensation is getting significant attention in the media today is gender pay parity. Pay parity is all about ensuring that women and men earn the same pay for the same work. It's easy to believe that in a world as advanced as ours, this kind of concept should no longer be an issue. Yet the gender pay gap is still alive and well. Sources vary but an estimate from the World Economic Forum of the global pay gap puts it at 32 per cent. Factoring in countries around the world, we see that for every dollar a man earns, a woman earns 68 cents (Schwab *et al*, 2017).[4] This number varies depending on the geographic area, and only four regions are identified in the report as having gender pay gaps less than 30 per cent: Western Europe (25 per cent), North America (28 per cent), Central Europe and Eastern Asia (29 per cent) and Latin America and the Caribbean (29.8 per cent). The report looks at progress against pay parity year over year and estimates it would take about 100 years to close the gaps for good at the current rate of change.

In a story highlighting the practical impacts, Salesforce has made several very public pay adjustments in the last few years to correct gender pay equity (Dickey, 2018).[5] As a fast-growing company, the approach the firm has taken is laudable. When the leaders realize there's a pay gap, they make moves to fix it. However, after the first adjustment back in 2015, the firm realized it hadn't fixed the underlying factors with job offers and promotions, which meant the issues reappeared after some time. I highlight this because it's a major challenge for all employers to contend with, but there is hope that systems driven by AI would enable us to minimize or eliminate this pay gap. In this case, what if an AI was continuously scanning the compensation rates across the employee population and highlighting red flags or potential issues? In the case of Salesforce, it could even scan for these kinds of imbalances between men and women that would require massive payouts to rectify. In the case study below, I highlight an employer that uses an algorithm to assign work tasks and pay rates along with the results of the (ongoing) practice. It's an interesting story not just because it shows the usage of an algorithm in action, but because the results of the activity were still not exactly what the employer expected.

CASE STUDY Does AI ensure pay parity?

As we've discussed, one benefit of artificial intelligence is a system that makes decisions without bias or regard for someone's gender. Therefore, if you could design a system that schedules work shifts and pay rates based on a blind algorithm that does not factor gender into the decision, you would logically expect to find that men and women earn the same in such a system, correct?

But what if I told you this isn't the case? There's an employer that exists in markets around the globe, and in a recent analysis by economists from Stanford and the University of Chicago, they found that in spite of this highly automated, gender-blind algorithm that sets pay rates and assigns work in real time, men still out-earn women. This employer, if you're curious, is Uber. In an analysis released in 2018, several economists looked at the transactions that occurred in the system to understand if there was a pay gap (Cook *et al*, 2018).[6] Transparently, one of the economists admitted that he fully expected to see little to no gap in pay because of the structure of the system. Again, we all logically expect this. Yet the conclusions of the analysis are equally logical, if a little confounding, for those of us that had hoped to find a mechanism for eliminating the gender pay gap.

The gender pay gap for Uber drivers is 7 per cent, and the gap is explained by three key factors. First, experience accounts for about 33 per cent of the gap. To put it simply, drivers with more trips earn more than drivers with fewer trips. Because men have longer tenures on the Uber platform, on average, they reap the benefits of this. Drivers who have taken more than 2,500 trips earn an average of $3 per hour more than those drivers with less than 100 trips. Second, driving speed accounts for about 50 per cent of the difference. Men drive faster, which means they can get more pickups per hour. Men drive marginally faster on average in the broader population as well. Third, variations in work times and routes make up the remaining 17 per cent. Men take on shifts during higher surge times and in surge-friendly locations, leading to higher hourly earnings. Surges occur when there is higher demand for drivers than the available supply, which pushes up the cost per drive for passengers.

It's worthwhile to note the gap is better than what we'd find in the open market, and it's explainable, too. What is important is that pay *assignments are equal*. Men and women that drive the same route at the same time earn the same pay. In that respect the algorithm really is levelling the playing field. However, in terms of hourly wages, men are earning slightly more because they have more experience, faster driving speeds and more lucrative routes/pickups. The logical conclusion after reviewing this information is that unequal results don't necessarily point to unequal treatment at the outset. In this case the algorithm worked exactly as advertised, and human unpredictability explains the rest.

Benefits administration

'Alexa, what amount of my deductible has been met?'

We have already discussed the importance of voice-interactive systems and the value they bring to users, but they also pose a new frontier for benefits conversations. In an interview, benefits executive Richard Silberstein pointed out that the benefits profession is on the verge of being disrupted by technologies enabled by artificial intelligence (Albinus, 2018).[7] His belief is that the technology will allow us to go beyond the traditional 'open enrolment meeting' focal point where a human is required to explain and explore benefit options to individuals in the workplace. While that human touch is still a part of the process and will not completely go away, the value of having more personalized discussions with individual workers cannot be overlooked.

Even if we don't always like to admit it, each of us wants to feel special. We want to be treated uniquely. One area of the business and how employees interact that demands a level of personalization is in benefits selection and administration. Representing up to 40 per cent of an employee's cost on top of their salary, benefits make up a major line item in every company's budget (Hadzima, 2005).[8] That's precisely why we need to be sure that our approach to benefits ensures that every single employee gets the most beneficial option that fits their unique needs, and one of the best ways to do that on a micro or macro level is through communication. The use cases for employee benefits communications are fairly broad, and I've seen personally what happens when you throw all of the options and information at all of the people; they have some level of paralysis due to the information overload and either select a default option or just maintain course, even if other options might be better suited to their needs and lifestyle. But we can change this, and it isn't difficult. For instance, maybe you define your communications based around employee age group:

- Offering childcare options to baby boomers is a missed opportunity for impact. Instead, offering prescription drug benefits or long-term care coverage would be more appealing for that particular audience.

- Gen Xers – dependent care coverage, retirement planning assistance, elder care assistance, or college planning for young children.
- Millennials – student loan repayment programmes, financial wellness training/assistance or coaching for first-time healthcare insurance buyers.

When HR leaders stop and think logically about this, it makes perfect sense. Different parts of the employee population have different needs at different times. This idea of communicating proactively is something that healthcare firm HealthJoy weaves into its approach to the market. The company's bot will reach out to members at strategic times of the year to remind them to get a flu shot. However, unlike a generic message or text reminder, the system also automatically scans insurance information to find the best local provider. For those with company-sponsored insurance, it advises users on which providers are covered by the insurance plan, and for those with national healthcare offerings it might simply suggest a local provider based on customer reviews and ratings. This kind of personalized, tailored outreach would have never happened if it required a human to manage the process, but allowing an algorithm to run this costs the company virtually nothing and may reduce costs and expenses associated with presenteeism (coming to work while sick).

One AI scientist even envisions a future where some of the common employee assistance programme (EAP) or even well-being benefits are being handled by an algorithm (Shutan, 2017).[9] EAP plans are notorious for being rolled out by companies with much fanfare only to have little to no adoption among the employee population. This scientist believes chatbots could serve as basic therapists, trainers or assistants to help bridge the gap between employee needs and a human response. On the wellness side of the equation, instead of paying for personal trainers for workers, the bot could easily serve as a coach for basic nutrition advice, exercise and more. The cost for the employer would be virtually nothing per interaction, but research shows that increases in employee mental and physical health (and the accompanying reductions in undue stress) can improve their workplace performance (Gino, 2016).[10]

For companies, there are other opportunities on the benefits front that might be challenging to manage with human labour. Employers with self-funded insurance plans might use algorithms to target recurring medical issues or trends that are driving up plan costs, seeking alternatives to reduce those specific types of issues as needed. Or it could be about making sure people actually adopt the programmes and benefits the company is already paying for, keeping their satisfaction high with their offerings and making sure they maintain their health to the degree possible. It's no stretch of the imagination to imagine bots helping with that adoption rate similar to how we discussed bots helping with technology adoption rates earlier in this book. Instead of giving a worker 200 pages of documents and expecting the person to make a choice about what benefits fit their needs, a bot could assist each person with their questions, unique circumstances and budget to help them find the best solution. On top of that, it could also follow up throughout the year to support adoption and ongoing usage of the selected benefits. For example:

> 'Mary, if you remember, you signed up for the flexible spending account to save money for medical expenses but you haven't yet taken advantage of that. Those funds expire at the end of the year so be sure to use your flex spending debit card when you're paying for covered expenses like copays and deductibles. If you don't have your card, I can replace that for you or I can get you the reimbursement form if that's easier for you to use.'

Again, this would cost nothing but would potentially increase Mary's satisfaction with her benefits because she is able to take full advantage of what she and the company are paying for. Alternatively, the system could work the same way but in a reverse or look-back scenario:

> 'Jamie, I see that you spent $1,700 out of pocket this year for medical expenses. Did you know that could have been tax-free under one of our medical savings account options? If you like, I can help you learn more about those options for the coming plan year.'

David Contorno, a benefits broker, has seen the implementation of AI into programmes like telemedicine increase utilization by 25 times simply because the system can be more personalized and interactive with each individual person (Ramos, 2017).[11] If you're not familiar, telemedicine is an option where employees can call or video chat with a doctor instead of having to visit a doctor's office for some routine issues: ear infections, pink eye, sinus issues and so on. The cost is dramatically lower for both the employee and the employer than an actual doctor's visit, and the physician can even prescribe antibiotics and other medications without requiring an in-person visit. These programmes are incredibly efficient uses of benefits resources, but they don't always have high adoption rates by employees because they forget about it or they are unsure how to use the benefit. The cost saved is approximately $100 per virtual session or use versus visiting a doctor in person, even if we don't account for the issues associated with driving to the office and waiting in an overcrowded room, potentially exposing ourselves to other germs in the process (Wike, 2014).[12] Now, imagine expanding that cost saving across your employee population thanks to the value and scalability of AI technologies and you'll start to see Contorno's vision for the companies he works with.

Employee self-service

The value promise of employee self-service has long been that workers can handle some of their own tasks without having to involve HR in the process, giving HR teams more time to dedicate to non-administrative, or strategic, actions. If that sounds familiar, it should – it is the same overall value promise of AI for HR leaders as discussed earlier in this book.

When I think about the kinds of questions I answered as an HR specialist in my early days, a significant portion of them were repeated over and over again. How do I change a beneficiary? How do I roll over a retirement plan? How do I check my vacation leave balance? These kinds of questions were repeated on an almost daily basis by employees, and a tool that would have enabled them to get those answers more quickly and consistently while saving me time to do other activities would have been incredibly valuable.

The concept of self-service has been around for as long as HR teams have adopted technologies that allow user inputs from outside the HR team, but don't assume that this is a common staple of all employers, even large ones. In one Infor case study exploring the use of technology at Pilot Flying J, an operator of travel centres and rest stops, the company's CIO Mike Rogers discussed the firm's adoption of a cloud-based HR technology suite.[13] Rogers explained that his company's 27,000 employees had been using paper forms and fax machines to handle even simple employee address changes up to that point. This represented a major frustration for workers and in a high-turnover industry, even the smallest details could lead to a more broadly negative employee experience. The company's goal was to reduce turnover by half by adopting new HR systems to reduce that level of friction.

While anecdotal, this represents a common challenge for employers worldwide. How do we serve the needs of a population without completely overwhelming our HR infrastructure and resources? This is a perfect opportunity for bots to support employee needs, extending the capabilities of the existing human resources function and enabling a more consistent, high-touch employee experience. When it comes to the employee experience, there are a variety of lenses to look through: cultural, physical and even technological. One company that focuses on creating a frictionless employee experience from an IT perspective is Credit Suisse. The financial services firm headquartered in Zurich has nearly 50,000 employees, plus a special one called Amelia. When workers have issues with passwords, logging into their systems, and other routine issues, they reach out to Amelia for help. Just like a normal IT help desk, Amelia can work with employees to resolve their issue and get them back to work. However, Amelia has the benefit of being able to serve multiple employees at the same time, regardless of time zones, and she doesn't require overtime pay. Why? Because Amelia is a chatbot, and this bot is designed to scale up support for common IT issues to keep employees from being frustrated by minor IT annoyances and to help the internal IT team focus on more important issues than password resets and such.

This type of employee self-service, where workers partner with an automated assistant, is becoming increasingly common, whether in IT, in HR, or in other areas of the business. Smart HR teams will look at these assistants not just as a tool designed to solve a narrow set of problems, but as an additional resource on the team. Just like junior staffers often have tasks delegated to them that are not worth the time investment for more senior workers, bots and automated assistants fill that same role for an HR team.

Spoke is one firm that offers these automated assistants for human resources teams. The CEO, Jay Srinivasan, believes that these tools have the ability to support not just enterprise HR teams, but small departments of one as well (Banerjee, 2018).[14] Having run HR functions as a small team of me, myself and I in the early days of my career, I know all too well how easy it is to get bogged down in the details and never take on the more strategic, forward-looking aspects of the job. Srinivasan says that employee self-service tools are commonly marketed towards larger firms, but small companies have the same basic needs around task management, ticketing and support. Spoke's team has seen that nearly half of all questions that are submitted to HR teams could be answered immediately and automatically by an algorithm, requiring no downtime or lost productivity for the HR team. Another interesting point about Spoke is that it has adopted a Slack-like pricing model, where customers only pay for the active users in the system each month, not a set number of seats or licenses. Why does that matter? Because this is a major incentive for Spoke to make the product incredibly easy to use for employees, driving adoption and usage.

Another example of an employer that uses HR self-service chatbots is E W Scripps. Founded in 1878, the firm's 4,000 employees rely on an automated tool to support their daily needs. Employees who use the chat interface can get access to multiple systems at one time, because the chatbot is connected with the company's HR case management, workforce management, benefits and HRIS systems. If an employee needed answers from several places that could take some time to log in to each system, navigate the interface and find the solution. However, since the bot is integrated with multiple systems at once, the employees can get that information at their fingertips using natural language queries instead of trying to figure out where to navigate in a system they don't use very often.

Diversity and harassment

In a world shaken by the #MeToo movement, there is an incredibly heightened awareness of diversity, harassment and compliance. Interestingly, both of the companies we'll examine below were co-founded by women and both have goals to reduce bias and discrimination in the workplace.

The first of the two is Spot, co-founded by Julia Shaw, a criminal psychologist and memory expert at University College London. The tool uses a chatbot to interview workers about their harassment experience and then can submit the anonymous report to a trusted person within the company. Interestingly, this can be used to help circumvent HR within the process, despite HR often being the default 'first stop' in the reporting mechanism for any discrimination or harassment issues. This is intentionally designed that way for a few reasons: first, it avoids the discomfort of being identified and making a complaint in person, and second, the unemotional interactive chatbot may help to draw out more accurate information from complainants as they recount their experiences.

This concept is a valuable one, because it takes advantage of the flexibility and always-on nature of chatbots and combines it with the need to approach a situation without any preconceived notions or defensiveness. In the highly publicized 2017 events that led to uproars about gender discrimination in the workplace, several of the stories included a variation of, 'I went to HR but nothing was done about my situation.' If this type of tool can help to alleviate harassment for even a single person, it should be considered a success. However, the adoption and usage could surprise those of us that know how often harassment allegations typically go unmentioned. According to one interview, Shaw said that within just a few weeks of making the tool freely available to the public, it had been used more than 200 times (Olson, 2018).[15]

The second tool that is targeting bias in the workplace is doing so in a slightly different manner. Joonko, named for Junko Tabei, the first woman to reach the summit of Mount Everest in 1975, is a real-time diversity coach that utilizes machine learning and natural language processing to identify and uncover biases, whether conscious or unconscious. In practical terms, the system plugs into existing HR software to get a snapshot of the workforce as it currently stands. It can then start making recommendations based on areas to improve. For example, maybe recruiting pipelines are not very diverse, which will have a cumulative negative effect on company diversity in the long run. While we'll explore other types of recruiting tools in the next chapter, this is one example of how diversity blends over into other areas of the function and the business. On the company's website, visitors can see a short demonstration of how Joonko's AI can automatically flag various words and phrases in a Slack chat conversation, encouraging users to find other, more suitable terms to share their thoughts. It's early yet for this particular startup, but as other use cases emerge one can only imagine that these types of tools will find a greater foothold in the workplace environment.

AI-enabled workforce planning

One of the more complex elements that spans workforce management, talent analytics and business impact is workforce planning. Many employers struggle with this process. Even if they have a handle on current hiring needs, few firms have the practices and structure in place to be able to predict demand for specific types of talent and skills into the future. However, some firms are seeing AI give them the edge in this process (D'Onforio, 2018).[16]

By analysing a variety of supply sources for talent, businesses can predict where their talent is most likely to come from. Consider for a moment where your candidates might be found: social networking sites, applicant tracking systems, university databases and more. Employers can pool these various inputs to create a massive database of information about employment trends and sources.

They can then use machine learning algorithms to develop workforce planning models. There may be trends in sources that aren't obvious to the naked eye, but an algorithm might be able to shed light on those with ease. The other side of the equation is around talent and skill demand. How does the employer know what it will need? Part of this comes from analysing business context and goals. If the company plans to pursue a new type of technology development, those skills that apply to that technology field will become increasingly prioritized in the workforce planning model.

Matching up the supply and demand sounds simple, but the reality is it takes a significant amount of work. The positive side to this conversation is that AI can take away much of the struggle and stress that this process has historically involved. Instead of relying on a spreadsheet and pivot tables to analyse reams of data, employers can leverage smart algorithms to identify opportunities and trends that exist to hire the right people at the right time for the right task.

What I hope you're left with here is the idea that some of the more mundane and/or unpleasant administrative functions of HR are at the cusp of automation. And the promise of automation in these areas is greater time availability for important tasks like hiring, training and engaging the workforce. Because of the transactional nature of the tasks and activities covered in this chapter combined with the high cost of errors, these will be some of the first areas to be significantly impacted by artificial intelligence technologies; however, they won't be the last.

Key points

- Payroll, workforce management and benefits administration all share common characteristics: highly routine, high volume and high cost of errors. This makes them ripe for disruption by artificial intelligence.

- Offloading tasks from HR teams to the employees themselves using self-service and chatbots can free up HR staff to focus on more critical pieces of the business.

- Employers can't focus on actions like hiring and training until they have ironed out the issues around core HR and workforce management. Only then can they move on to more strategic activities.

Notes

1 https://www.youtube.com/watch?v=jN6UKJhuAno

2 https://www.replicon.com/time-intelligence/

3 http://www.aptituderesearchpartners.com/2018/03/07/why-im-passionate-about-payroll/

4 http://www3.weforum.org/docs/WEF_GGGR_2017.pdf

5 https://techcrunch.com/2018/04/17/salesforce-spent-another-2-7-million-to-adjust-pay-gaps-related-to-race-and-gender/

6 https://web.stanford.edu/~diamondr/UberPayGap.pdf

7 https://www.benefitnews.com/news/ai-poised-to-transform-open-enrollments

8 http://web.mit.edu/e-club/hadzima/how-much-does-an-employee-cost.html

9 https://www.employeebenefitadviser.com/news/ais-brave-new-world-of-insurance-apps

10 https://hbr.org/2016/04/are-you-too-stressed-to-be-productive-or-not-stressed-enough

11 https://venturebeat.com/2017/10/24/ai-is-making-employee-benefits-a-little-more-beneficial/

12 https://www.healthitoutcomes.com/doc/telehealth-costs-up-to-less-than-office-visits-0001

13 https://pages.infor.com/hfe-hcm-case-study-pilot-flying-j-cis.html?cid=NA-NA-HCA-US-HCM-0716-FY17-HCM-Assets-WWCS-43525

14 https://www.hrtechnologist.com/interviews/employee-self-service/interview-with-jay-srinivasan-ceo-at-spoke/

15 https://www.forbes.com/sites/parmyolson/2018/03/02/chatbot-spot-sexual-harassment-ai/#1bff2fc84a51

16 https://www.hrtechnologist.com/articles/recruitment-onboarding/how-a-telecoms-giant-is-using-ai-to-predict-its-future-workforce-needs/

Talent acquisition

05

The date is March 2017. The place is Austin, Texas. The audience is on the edge of their seats waiting to hear the results. Who would win: the top sourcing experts or the algorithm?

The SourceCon Grandmaster Challenge is well known in the sourcing industry, but others outside the field might not be familiar with this competition. The contest for 2017 was fairly straightforward: download a folder containing three job descriptions, download a batch of 5,000 resumes and examine the resumes to determine who was actually sourced, interviewed and hired. In other words, contestants would review skills from the resumes and predict which of the individuals made it through an actual hiring process. Points were given in each case for selecting the right resumes and their classifications (interviewed, hired, etc). At the same time as the humans, a piece of AI-driven technology from Brilent was also attempting to solve the riddle. Spoiler alert: the humans won, but it was a tempered victory. We'll talk more about the process, the results and the practical implications in the sourcing section below, but this epic battle is the perfect lead into the conversation about how AI tools fit into the recruiting function.

Talent acquisition is often practised by HR professionals that have a measure of innovative thinking and a healthy appreciation for getting results. They also have low rules orientation – this essentially means they are less interested in following a policy manual and instead seek autonomy in how they accomplish their work. For example, most companies don't have a recruiting 'manual' that tells how and where to find candidates. Instead, recruiters are often a little bit like scientists, tweaking, testing and experimenting with their tools and skills to find the right candidate for the job.

The above-referenced competition is a great example of how this plays out in real life. This combination of factors has led to a proliferation of recruiting applications using artificial intelligence technologies. Because the role of a recruiter is more routine than, say, an HR business partner, the recruiting function is more easily supported by automation technologies. Consider the typical workflow for a job: the requisition opens, candidates apply, candidates are assessed, candidates are screened and somewhere down the line the candidate actually talks to a recruiter or hiring manager. All of those early steps are opportunities to leverage chatbots, automated screening tools and other systems to scale the interactions with candidates.

On top of that, the hiring process generates an immense amount of data, one of the other core foundational underpinnings discussed earlier in this book. Because data privacy and security are such critical points for many employers, these topics are highlighted in detail in Chapter 8. If a company hires 500 workers per year and receives 5,000 job applications, those 500 that were chosen as well as the 4,500 that were not create some opportunities to understand trends and gather insights on the types of workers and skills a company desires. This ratio of applicants to openings is a conservative figure, as some estimates put the average number of applications per job opening at 250 (Sullivan, 2013).[1] Regardless, the data tell a compelling story about how companies hire and can shed light on what can be done to improve the process.

The pressure to interact with and support each applicant has also been driven by a shift in demand in recent years. Today, candidates expect greater responsiveness and transparency from employers than ever before. In one of the world's leading candidate experience research publications, the 2017 TalentBoard Candidate Experience Research Report, the authors recommended giving candidates similar experiences to consumer shopping where they can see their progress or understand how long the process might take before undertaking the application steps.[2] While technologies have given companies more opportunities to scale their recruiting practices, they have also been known to incense candidates that apply to many jobs without a response. In reality it takes only a few minutes to let candidates know they are not chosen for a position, but many employers still don't utilize that functionality in their applicant tracking systems. It's rare to go to a recruiting event and not hear about the 'black hole', the descriptor given by many to the applicant tracking systems where resumes are dumped in but no communication is ever returned. This greater desire for transparency means the stakes are higher than ever for employers that want to attract and hire the right talent.

Additionally, a greater focus on diversity in today's business climate also increases the perceived value of automated systems. One use case is resume blinding, where the name or other identifying information is removed from the resume to prevent conscious or unconscious bias. In one study, applicants with white-sounding names like 'Emily' or 'Greg' received nearly 50 per cent more callbacks than candidates with black-sounding names like 'Lakisha' or 'Jamal' (Bertrand and Mullainathan, 2004).[3] In the context of the study, the researchers found that having a white-sounding name is worth as much as eight years of work experience. The practical implication of this for purposes of the AI discussion is that a piece of technology should, theoretically, reduce the bias in the process by focusing on work experience, skills, or other non-discriminatory factors. As we'll see in some of the examples within this chapter, some of the technology providers in the space are also taking alternative approaches to reduce any bias in the process from the earliest resume screens all the way through to the interview process.

One other comment on diversity that has been particularly intriguing in the research process for this book: many of the startup firms in the HR technology industry are founded by women, and while not all of them try to tackle the same problem or step in the process, several of these businesses have a distinct approach for minimizing bias and discrimination. The list is long and varied, but I'll give you a glimpse (in Table 5.1) into a sampling of the types of tools that are being developed (several of which will be explored in this chapter).

Table 5.1 A sampling of female HR technology founders with AI-based recruiting technology

Name	Company	Focus
Athena Karp	HiredScore	Screening and matching candidates in an unbiased way
Kristen Hamilton	Koru	Candidate assessments
Frida Polli	Pymetrics	Gamified candidate assessments
Kieran Snyder	Textio	Augmented writing tool to minimize bias in job ads
Laura Mather	Talent Sonar	Structured interviews to remove hiring bias
Stacey Chapman	Swoop Talent	Integration service to unify talent data sources

Sourcing tools and technologies

Sourcing candidates is one of the most data-heavy aspects of recruiting. Consider the process a sourcer or recruiter often uses to find talent, the various systems that data can be stored in, and the stages of communication that exist, and you'll quickly understand why sourcing is the low-hanging fruit of the talent acquisition world. A normal recruiter spends an inordinate amount of time sourcing, the act of combing through resumes and connecting with potential candidates. Having tools on hand to sift through the massive amounts of data is highly valuable.

External sourcing is what recruiters typically mean when they talk about recruiting. This isn't about posting a job and waiting for candidates – it's about going out and finding the right talent wherever it might be. Let's revisit the SourceCon Grandmaster Challenge. In this instance, the contestants were attempting to find the right people for fictional roles. As you recall, the humans won the competition, but the AI-driven tool was not far behind. In the end, sourcing expert Randy Bailey was crowned champion and another set of contestants tied for second place. The algorithm produced by Brilent came in third place, but it only required 3.2 seconds to deliver results, while the humans spent anywhere from 4 to 25 hours to research their submissions (Stroud, 2017).[4] This story is a powerful testament to the value that both parties bring to the conversation. In his review of the competition, sourcing expert Jim Stroud mentioned that the humans that won or placed highly in the competition used technology to narrow down the resumes, but ultimately relied on human intuition or 'their gut' to make decisions at the end of the process. In essence, there is a spectrum from totally human to totally algorithmic, and the best value and performance lies somewhere in the middle of that range. Let's take a look at some of the technologies that enable great recruiting performance today.

Examples of automated sourcing technologies run the gamut from databases connected to smart search tools such as those offered by HiringSolved to automated recruiting solutions like Envoy offered by Entelo, with a variety of other 'flavours' of technology in between. The core thread these various tools share is the blend of intuition and technology that enables performance greater than the sum of their parts.

Take the sourcing and search tools offered, for example. When recruiters search a database for a specific set of software development skills, they may or may not be aware of related skills and competencies that would also be relevant to the search. For instance, software development might be a top-level skill, but underneath that are dozens of variations and specialities, from software testing to front-end development. Because the system has processed resumes from candidates with those skills, it knows when to suggest other, related skills that might also help in a search. This may not hold a ton of value for senior recruiters with a lot of experience – after all, they probably already know the primary and secondary skills as well as common recruiting channels from companies to universities to interest groups. However, for more junior recruiters and non-technical HR professionals, those types of capabilities have the potential to dramatically improve recruiting results, lower cycle times and improve that all-important hiring manager relationship. While searching candidate databases and using Boolean search tactics have been mainstays of recruiting for some time, the real shift here is that algorithms can infer skills matches in a way that humans simply can't. For clarity, Boolean search is the process of searching a database using operators to narrow search results. For example, if you search in a database for 'software engineer' but also use '-Java' you can filter out any software engineer resumes with Java in them. More complex Boolean logic can give more accurate results.

A different option on the sourcing front is today's slate of automated sourcing and contact tools. In late 2017 Entelo unveiled its Envoy solution, designed to help busy recruiters reach out to more candidates in a scalable, automated fashion. The common method for sourcing candidates for a role is this: you post the job, you go to a database, you search for candidates, you contact those promising candidates, you follow up with any candidates via phone to move the ball forward and potentially seal the deal. In reality, this is incredibly time-consuming. For highly technical roles I've filled in the past, the sourcing phase could take anywhere from 8 to 30 hours per position or more, depending on just how specialized it was. Sourcing technologies attempt to shorten that chain by automating a few of the more time-consuming aspects. Using this software, recruiters post a position, then they take a well-deserved break. In all seriousness, the technology picks up after the search criteria are identified, automatically finding candidates in the database that are likely matches for the skills and automatically reaching out to them on your behalf. Any warm or responsive contacts are then transitioned to the recruiter for a more 'human' touch. Ask any recruiter and they'll tell you the early parts of the sourcing process are fairly straightforward if you know how to search and make contact with candidates. The actual high-value conversations don't come until later, but without having a solid funnel of candidates there will be no opportunities to have those high-value interactions.

Another example of technology developing in the sourcing world is what the team at Restless Bandit calls 'talent rediscovery'. One of several companies that offers this type of approach, the basic idea is in rediscovering the valuable connections you already have in your own database before paying to find candidates elsewhere through job boards, job ads, or other methods. Think for a moment about your applicant tracking system (ATS), if you have one. How many resumes are in there relative to the number of positions you've posted over time? Using the estimate of 250 applications per posting from earlier in this chapter, a company that has posted 100 jobs has more than 25,000 resumes in its database. One problem with this is that of those 25,000 resumes, maybe only 18,000 of them are unique; the rest are duplicate applications by the same person for different jobs. Yet another problem? Stale data. Information on those resumes, if it's left to stagnate over a few years, may be virtually worthless in some cases. People change jobs. They relocate. They change contact information. Without updated information, those resumes lose their value over time. Therefore, these systems rely on an algorithm, which sits on top of the applicant tracking system collecting data on hiring patterns and which candidates ultimately succeed in the selection process. This feature can quickly analyse a database of prior applicants and resurface the ones that are most relevant to the current requisition. Logically, because these are candidates that have already applied to the company at some point in the past, it's possible that they might be a 'warmer' audience than those available through other typical sourcing channels and cold outreach. Clients of these firms are able to rediscover candidates buried within the applicant tracking system to fill new requisitions, saving time and resources to locate new applicants.

Other opportunities on the sourcing front are more process-oriented, though still incredibly valuable as many firms have poorly defined and/or poorly refined recruiting processes. For example, Beamery, a UK-based recruitment candidate relationship management (CRM) platform, also brings value to the sourcing conversation. The company's tools not only help to automate the applicant ranking process – they also support interactions with candidates. For instance, if recruiters fail to follow up with a high-value applicant, the system can trigger an automated reminder to get the applicant back on the recruiter's radar. Because timing is critical in recruiting, the technology can also suggest the most valuable time to reach out and connect with candidates. Finally, recruiters can leverage machine learning-powered data matching and automation systems to help them prioritize the candidates that are most engaged and are the best fit for open and future roles.

Finally, no sourcing conversation would be complete without a mention of LinkedIn, one of the default tools for virtually every recruiting shop. At the end of the day, large players like LinkedIn are sitting on a stockpile of data that can be leveraged along with AI to create powerful tools and recommendations for employers looking to hire the best talent. Additionally, they are often the first stop for recruiters and sourcers looking to find the right candidates not just because they have amassed large numbers of users, but because their search algorithms are fundamental in narrowing those pools of users to the right candidates.

LinkedIn's Recruiter tool uses a variety of machine learning to power its recommendation engine. Beyond the typical resume keyword search, the system can analyse a wide spectrum of information to find and deliver the right candidates to a recruiter. Interestingly, one newer signal that the company has brought to the product is candidate receptivity. This has a double benefit of prioritizing people who might be open to contact about jobs and deprioritizing those who are not, improving the user experience within the platform. By analysing a wide spectrum of behaviours, the system can surface individuals in searches that are more likely to be receptive to a contact from a recruiter. Some questions the algorithm considers in its recommendations of candidate openness to recruiter contact are:

- How responsive has the individual been to recruiter contact in the past?
- How responsive has the individual been to contact with various types of recruiters, companies, or industries?
- Is there any specific, recent job search activity?
- Are there any connection activities or trends apparent and what might they signify?

This approach could help to improve hiring outcomes for employers. Employer branding is focused on getting the company's culture and information out into the market so candidates can be aware of the firm and its available jobs. It logically follows that candidates who share, comment, or interact with a company online are much more likely to respond to contact from a recruiter. If algorithms push those types of individuals higher in recruiter searches, that should lead to better, more targeted contacts, conversations and hires. Additionally, with news in 2017 that both Google and Microsoft have entered the small and mid-size business (SMB) market with hiring solutions, it's not a stretch to imagine some of those tools making use of the existing AI infrastructure in these technology firms to make talent acquisition more predictive and analytical. For instance, at the 2016 Microsoft Ignite user conference, CEO Satya Nadella showed the audience the integration of its Cortana AI with LinkedIn data to help someone planning a meeting to better understand the attendees by visiting their LinkedIn profiles. Additionally, the Google Jobs initiative to bring an AI-powered search experience for candidates is another example of a single step with far-reaching impacts.

While not an exhaustive list, these examples pretty clearly demonstrate the type of value that AI can bring to sourcing. As one of the most labour-intensive elements in the entire HR spectrum, talent acquisition professionals stand to gain much from the adoption of AI-based recruiting technologies. However, as we all know, simply sourcing candidates isn't enough. We need to be able to match, screen and hire the right ones as well.

CASE STUDY Automated job offers: fantasy or reality?

If a recent graduate applies for a software engineering role in one of the company's competitive markets, the algorithm pushes the candidate through a series of short assessments to understand coding skill levels and personal characteristics. If the candidate scores above a certain threshold, a job offer is generated automatically without any interview being required.

Note that in this entire process, not a single human interaction occurred, and nobody from the company was involved in screening in any form or fashion. This sounds like a futuristic version of recruiting, but this example of an Amazon hiring experiment was mentioned in *HR Magazine* in June 2016 (Lee, 2016).[5] For many companies, this sounds like a somewhat frightening concept. After all, who offers a job to a person they've never met or even spoken with? However, from an objective standpoint, this is an incredible solution to some of the problems that have plagued the workplace for some time. For example:

- The offer was made at market rates with no regard for salary history. Questions about salary history have been recently banned in several US states to improve pay equality (HR Dive, 2018).[6]

- The offer was made regardless of the individual's race, country of origin, gender, etc. This effectively removes any bias from the hiring process.

- The person was reviewed objectively with a targeted assessment, ensuring that core skills are apparent and that the applicant was not able to get the job merely by performing well in the interview, socially or otherwise.

More practically, the experimental solution was put in place to solve a more pressing factor: the time required to interview, evaluate and offer a job to a candidate. In tight labour markets, time means lost opportunity in many cases, and the fastest hiring process of all requires no human interaction.

While it's still early, future advances on this type of approach could include a few additional pieces of automation. For instance, what if the workflow looked something like this upon receiving a candidate's application:

- the job is historically difficult to fill;

- the position has had no qualified applicants to date;

- the candidate's resume meets the basic skill requirements for the role.

The near-instantaneous analysis complete, the firm's recruiting system supplies a short assessment to the candidate to determine basic skills proficiency in the specific role. Upon the satisfactory completion of the assessment with high marks, the system automatically generates an offer letter to the candidate at the current market rate.

While most of us are not ready for this level of sophisticated automation in the hiring process, we can all agree that it diminishes the biases that plague hiring decisions in virtually every company around the world. It's a radical approach, but then again, it's a radical problem as well.

Candidate matching

Similar to sourcing, matching is another time- and labour-intensive activity for recruiters that can be best augmented by the right technology. Matching is the process of pairing applicants with jobs and ranking them based on their qualifications. In the past, most matching was done by simple resume keyword extraction. The more keywords you have in the resume, the higher you rate for job fit. While this isn't a bad place to start, there should be additional considerations in the process. As someone that has had to review keyword-stuffed resumes in the past for unqualified candidates, there has to be a better way to separate the wheat from the chaff.

This is also a critical point because as we get closer to an official hiring decision, companies would in theory be less and less comfortable with allowing AI to be the final say in the conversation. After all, at the end of the day the HR team and the hiring managers at the firm are the ones on the hook from a compliance standpoint for hiring decisions. Who's going to put an algorithm on trial for disparate impact or discriminatory hiring? For that reason, the closer we get to a hiring decision the more humans will interact with the systems to make a joint decision on the best candidates using the intuition both systems can offer.

An example of this comes in HireVue's video screening tools. Video interviews are often thought of only in the live conversational context, such as a live video chat between the candidate and the hiring team. In truth, many employers prefer to use asynchronous video interviews to examine candidates in addition to and as a precursor to those live interviews. Asynchronous videos are simply videos that have been recorded at a previous time and that may be played at any time. They are the opposite end of the spectrum from live video conversations where both parties must be present at the same time for discussion. HireVue's Insights score can consider a range of candidate factors to rate their 'performance' in a recorded interview. Considering things like tone, word use and even eye contact, systems like HireVue's allow employers to see candidate scores at a glance before deciding which to follow up with.

A similar video hiring tool, the mroads Paññā system, can score candidate video performance, using machine learning to listen and watch for aberrant behaviours. For instance, ways to cheat on a video interview might be listening to cues from someone offscreen or averting your eyes to read notes from a notepad. The mroads technology can see and hear those types of actions and flag them, allowing recruiters to double check on those video recordings to verify the content. Another interesting capability of the system is a quick assessment that candidates can take on screen or during the application process. If candidates apply for a technical job, the system can flash a quick coding quiz on the screen for the individual to complete, quickly demonstrating their capability with the programming language associated with the position. The system automatically scores the candidates on the questions upon submittal and ranks them in the dashboard so recruiters know which candidates to prioritize in their outreach.

In the matching phase, it's easy for humans to be swayed by a number of factors, whether consciously or unconsciously. As mentioned above, the resurgence of focus on diversity means technologies that support these decisions with data and evidence instead of 'gut feel' are going to become more and more valuable. A great example of this in action is the set of tools offered by HiredScore. When individuals apply, HiredScore captures their resume and application data. The system can quickly analyse and understand which applicants match the job requirements. Because this is a compliance-based system, it doesn't consider irrelevant factors and focuses on whether the person can actually meet the stated requirements of the job.

Simple concept, right? If a system can analyse inputs and match resumes with job postings, we can select the right people for the job. In reality, the problem that exists is that job postings and resumes tell distinctly different stories. One tells the story of the employer, describing the history, cultural elements and strategic direction. The other explains the career history of the applicant, demonstrating skills, roles and other accomplishments. Analysis of the resume can pull out key bits of information to match them with the job description, but it's not as simple as it sounds. The thing that users want most from a system like this is matching on an automated, ongoing basis with a thorough look not just at making it simple and easy but also at the compliance aspects. It shouldn't fall back on the HR or recruiting leader to see if bias or adverse impact is occurring – the system should be doing that analysis all along.

Assessments

Another consideration on the matching front involves assessments. Just as mroads and other video interviewing providers are incorporating assessments into the video screening process, other providers are exploring automating this as part of the standard application process. This includes firms like Koru, Pymetrics and Fortay. The latter offers a solution that aims to help companies scale their culture as they scale the business, one of the most common questions or challenges for fast-growing employers. While 'culture fit' is a loaded term in many HR circles, employers that understand some of the key competencies and behaviours that drive business results can leverage assessments to hire for those specific skills.

A quick word on 'culture fit', as some employers might get the wrong idea about this. Some companies are shy about the 'culture fit' conversation, because they have seen it used in a negative manner by hiring managers to block diverse candidates they didn't want to hire. However, good employers can still hire for key qualities that exist regardless of racial, gender, or other demographic lines. For instance, employers that place a high emphasis on customer service are not limited to any specific demographic group to find those qualities – the fundamental value exists in a very broad population. When I talk about culture fit, that's the concept I'm referring to.

Back to the technology discussion: Fortay's platform uses machine learning technology to define a firm's unique 'cultural fingerprint' based on ideal company values. Additionally, it examines and codifies cultural workplace attributes of the company's cultural champions, those who embody the key aspects of the firm's culture. This fingerprint is then used to assess relative cultural alignment in candidates to ensure a successful match and increased quality of hire. When clients use the system, they are able to improve the efficiency of the hiring process while simultaneously improving the quality of the candidate pipeline. For some clients, an unexpected benefit of leveraging Fortay was that it inherently enhanced the diversity of candidates by minimizing the potential of bias in the screening process for factors unrelated to the job or culture.

CASE STUDY Unilever uses AI for university hiring needs

When a company wants to hire students and recent graduates, they always do the same thing. The firm picks a university job fair, sends a recruiting team and collects paper resumes from attendees at the event. But the process is costly and the connection with results is somewhat tenuous. That's part of the reason Unilever decided to change its approach to campus recruiting by leveraging AI-driven assessments and video interviews (Feloni, 2017).[7]

The new screening method involved game-based assessments to examine candidates on a range of measures, including tolerance for risk. Existing employees took the assessments to create a benchmark to compare the candidates against, a concept known as concurrent validity. Concurrent validity helps employers to know if the scores candidates get on an assessment would match well with the characteristics and qualities of existing high performers on the team. Additionally, the video interviews were also AI-driven. Answers to the questions were analysed by an algorithm which considered body language, words and phrases used in conversation and tone of voice. The system then highlighted those candidates who were most qualified for the next step of the process, signifying the first time a candidate interacted with a recruiter at the firm.

The results have been incredibly impressive. After adopting the new technological approach, Unilever was able to hire its most diverse class ever, seeing a significant increase in minority applicants. Additionally, student hires came from more universities than ever before. Traditionally the company selected from just over 800 colleges, but the new crop of employees was hired from more than three times that many educational institutions (2,600). One of the most important metrics for any recruiting shop, time to fill dropped from four months to four weeks, saving an incredible amount of time both for candidates and the recruiters themselves.

Perhaps most importantly from a candidate experience perspective, a survey of 25,000 candidates showed a score equating to 82 per cent satisfaction, far beyond the typical satisfaction rates of most hiring processes for enterprise organizations. This just goes to show that increasing adoption of automation technologies doesn't have to lead to lower satisfaction from candidates – it can actually improve the results if approached strategically.

The role of data in recruiting

One thing is for certain after seeing just a small selection of the systems available to solve today's recruiting challenges: the future will be filled with more data and inputs from these types of systems than ever before, with many enterprise organizations juggling multiple systems due to geographic, business unit, or other specialized needs. But where does that data reside? Is there a way to connect it in a usable manner with organizational systems, or is it locked away as static information? That's the problem that systems like Swoop Talent are designed to solve. Swoop Talent is an example of a system that connects disparate data sources to allow employers to have a single, unified view of their talent and capabilities. While there are several systems in the market that can bring various data sources together, what's interesting about Swoop Talent is the wide variety of use cases, limited only by the imagination of the talent acquisition teams it supports. As an example, one interesting use case for the system is to target alumni, or former employees. Let's say a software developer resigns, is hired by the competition and begins gathering skills at another job. One to two years from now, that person is more valuable than they were when they left the role, correct? After all, the developer has most likely been learning and improving the requisite skills throughout that period of time. Eventually a position opens at the former employer that the person wouldn't have been a fit for. However, because the employer is using Swoop Talent, it can see from the updated talent profile (which pulls data from social sources like LinkedIn as well) that the individual now has the required skills necessary to perform the job. The recruiter can reach out to this person to start a discussion about returning to the new role. With research showing that returning employees are consistently a source of high-quality talent, it makes perfect sense as a recruiting strategy to recapture valuable workers even after they have left (Sullivan, 2014).[8] Swoop Talent's machine learning and predictive tools help to bring more information to recruiters so they can make better, well-informed decisions at the right time.

One final example while we're on the topic of data: IBM's new offering in the talent acquisition space is IBM Watson Recruitment.

The cognitive system increases recruiter efficiency by highlighting priorities that need attention. One way the system can use machine learning is to analyse applicant flow, previous recruiting funnel statistics and other signals to indicate whether a job is on or behind schedule from an applicant flow perspective. For instance, if it has taken three months and 50 candidates on average to find a suitable executive sales leader in the past, the system might flag the job if after a month it only has four or five candidates, far shy of the target needed to hit in order to stay on track with previous hiring cycles for the same role. Additionally, the system provides insight into which candidates are best qualified by automatically rating factors such as duration of experience in relevant roles, size of previous employers, college degree and major and more. However, this algorithm doesn't just march off on its own without support. Recruiters can actually rate the quality of the recommendations to help train the system to improve its suggestions over time. For example, if college degrees aren't relevant the recruiter can deprioritize that component while prioritizing experience at previous similar employers, which might be particularly relevant for this example of a sales executive. IBM is known as one of the frontrunners of leveraging AI in a variety of areas both inside and outside human capital management. The firm's Watson product is connected with so many other vendors via partnerships or integrations that it powers a surprising number of insights that we rely on in the HR space.

Recruiting applications for natural language processing

While we have explored the idea of natural language processing to some degree in a broader sense, it has some very interesting applications within the talent acquisition function. From augmented writing to skills analysis, employers have much to gain. As mentioned previously, most companies are sitting on an incredible amount of information that is just waiting to be tapped into. Tools that properly analyse that data, whether structured or unstructured, can help to illuminate insights and potential avenues to success.

One way employers can take advantage of NLP in recruiting is by analysing and understanding how to write the best job ads. One of the frontrunners in this space is Textio. Textio's augmented writing system is driven by examining more than 250 million job postings and their hiring outcomes. The analytics engine then delivers contextual help to recruiters by enabling them to craft better job ads. The system does this by instantly analysing job posting text content and predicting which words will have the best reception and impact on candidates. For instance, if the score appears as a 60 out of 100, the system flags words that might improve the score and performance of the ad, allowing recruiters to quickly and easily modify the content on the fly. For example, a single word may shift the perception of the ad to a more masculine or feminine nature, impacting the types of candidates that apply for the role. Because Textio knows the kinds of people that apply for jobs with similar wording, the predictions are incredibly precise.

The value promise of this type of tool is faster, more diverse hires of higher quality. This has become such a trusted asset for users that one client now requires all descriptions to be published with a minimum score of 90. Why so specific? It's because Textio's hiring data shows that jobs with a score of 90 or above are filling 17 per cent faster with up to 25 per cent more quality candidates in the pipeline. Trusted by enterprise hiring teams at Johnson & Johnson, Atlassian and other firms, the application gamifies the dull process of creating and posting job ads.

I expect to see other large software providers bringing these kinds of augmented writing technologies to their own platforms soon enough. As mentioned in an earlier chapter, when you can integrate these capabilities natively instead of having to access a different program or workflow to get your job done, you're more likely to take advantage of the technology. Technology adoption is always a challenging prospect, but even more so when it requires using multiple applications to get the job done.

In addition, these kinds of tools hold incredible promise to support better diversity and inclusion (D&I) outcomes. The way I've always explained it to executives is this: if you want to improve D&I, there's only so much wiggle room a company has to improve diversity once the employees have been hired. We can transfer and promote diverse workers, but if you have a homogeneous pool of candidates to work from at the front end of the hiring funnel, there's only so much advancement that can be made. For that reason, it's critical to make sure to keep diversity in mind during the job requisition development process, one of the earliest stages of the talent acquisition cycle.

Another natural language processing use case is focused on skills. In the explanation earlier in this chapter, I explained the challenge of matching resumes (candidate career history) with jobs (candidate skills). I talked about this from a company perspective of matching candidates with job openings, but there's actually value in the process for candidates as well. Imagine that you are looking for a job as a Vice President of Human Resources. You go to one of the job aggregator websites and create an alert to e-mail you with jobs that match your search criteria. Better matching technology means you'll only get alerts when jobs exist that are relevant and interesting to you. However, many of the tools in the market today will send regular e-mails even with irrelevant or incorrect job matches simply because one of the words in the job advertisement matched your search criteria. Fixing this problem helps to improve the candidate experience in a meaningful way. One fundamental way it approaches this is by translating jobs into actual skills, breaking down something as vague as a job title into the key skills associated with the position.

What if you were going to buy a vehicle but didn't know what the fair market value was for the specific model and feature set you were targeting? You know the basic details and ballpark price range, but how do you narrow in on a price that is specific to the vehicle you are looking for? More importantly, what if there was a system that gave you transparency into the pricing not just for the specific model, but for each individual feature you consider to be a high priority? One of the technologies in the market can do this today. Instead of relying purely on job titles to price open roles, which has been the common practice historically, the system allows users to see prevailing compensation rates for specific skill sets and helps to highlight and isolate the pricing impact of each.

As an example, users can price a job title and then start adding key skills one by one, viewing the cumulative impact on the cost of the role. This transparency might help users to realize that while it's always been listed as a requirement, one or two skills might not be necessary if they are pushing the cost of the role inordinately high. The practical implications on cost are staggering: one client using the system has accumulated more than $6 million in savings by streamlining and improving efficiencies in its approach to hiring. With an economy that is increasingly dependent on contingent labour, it's critical to consider that piece of the puzzle when pricing a job opening.

Chatbots as a communication mechanism

Chatbots offer incredible value and time savings for recruiters, and they also open up lines of communication with candidates in ways that humans simply can't without intense efforts of manual labour. Many of these tools in a recruiting context help to screen candidates at the top of the funnel, provide an interactive experience for applicants and keep recruiters updated in the back-end dashboard. In one demo, I actually had fun experimenting with the SMS-based interaction as the algorithm helped to schedule me for my 'interview' with the firm. It made me pause, because I knew in the process that this wasn't a person, but the bot served as a proxy for interpersonal contact in the recruiting process, which was good enough for me. Even though I wasn't applying for a real job and was just testing the technology, I have to imagine that users that are actually looking for work are going to enjoy the experience even more than I did.

The use case for bots in the talent acquisition process is straightforward: candidates interact with a chatbot instead of a person, allowing them to get instant help and attention and freeing up recruiters to focus on other activities. However, we're starting to see more automation in the process, opening up a world of innovative ideas. One example of unique usage of a recruiting bot was in automated screening of candidates for a complex role. In this instance, the ideal candidate for the job required a fairly significant following on social media to be qualified, so the bot asked the candidate about what social media platform was their most active and what their username or 'handle' was. The algorithm would then quickly scan the user account's posting consistency and recency to ensure that they met the minimum threshold for consideration. While the system also performed the standard interactive chat conversation with candidates, this step added additional value by automating a key part of the process, eliminating a time-consuming activity for the recruiting team to follow up and review the social media profiles of every potential candidate to ensure they had the necessary qualifications to move forward in the process.

One more example comes from Anna Ott, Head of the Startup Ecosystem for HR technology event UNLEASH (Ott, 2017).[9] In her story, she told about some of the surprising findings of adopting a chatbot for recruiting. For instance, candidates mostly interact with the bot outside of normal working hours. This means those applicants are getting attention when a recruiter would not typically be on staff, which is intriguing. The company's system, called 'hubbot', also received a wide range of questions beyond what was initially expected. Bots are programmed to respond to specific questions, which meant there were other queries outside its normal parameters it could not answer. If the question that comes in is not able to be matched to an answer in the database, hubbot sends the query directly to Ott, who answers it and then programs the response back into hubbot for future inquiries. The breakdown of questions from candidates probably wouldn't surprise any long-time recruiters, but it's intriguing nonetheless:

- salary 27 per cent;
- job specifics 24 per cent;
- company information 20 per cent;
- recruiting process 11 per cent;
- work culture and office environment 9 per cent;
- chatbot-related questions 7 per cent;
- general questions 2 per cent.

Ott's analysis of using the bot concluded with this valuable insight: employers can (and should) focus on being human while leveraging the advantages of bots to meet their hiring goals. In each of these examples of how AI is being used today within the recruiting sphere, it's clear that there is value in having these systems to help us engage with candidates, helping recruiters to save time for more valuable, timely tasks. This can include anything from recruiting high-priority roles to having conversations with key candidates in the pipeline, neither of which would be suitably offloaded to a bot, algorithm, or machine.

CASE STUDY How Anchor Trust leverages chatbots to drive recruiting

The Anchor Group is England's largest not-for-profit housing association, providing housing, care and support to people over 55 years old. The company's initiative was to create a better recruitment process, while providing the best applicant experience possible. Why? Because the firm noticed a pattern emerging during the recruitment follow-up process, with a high number of individuals that completed application forms then failing to engage with the in-house recruitment team despite attempts to reach them via phone and e-mail. Candidates' busy lifestyles meant that they were often unable to respond to e-mails or answer the phone (except at very specific times of the day) and tended to shy away from completing extensive application forms. The HR team also realized that there were highly skilled candidates that were experienced in care but unable to translate this onto paper in the form of a resume or CV.

The solution was a purpose-built recruitment chatbot built into Facebook Messenger, with questions that allowed Anchor Trust to screen and engage with candidates instantly. 1.2 billion people currently use Facebook Messenger and can access the tool straight from the mobile phone they keep in their pocket. This made it the perfect tool to build the new technology upon. When someone clicks on an ad on Facebook, a conversation will immediately open in Messenger, allowing the applicant to be qualified on a preliminary basis and booking in a specific time for a call with an Anchor recruiter.

Using the chatbot, Anchor Trust initiated automated one-on-one conversations with potential candidates. There are a variety of platforms available to build chatbots; however, Anchor chose to build its bot within FlowXO. The reason for this is because it has allowed the team to hard-code its own features and integrations, so that it can be much more than a simple automated question and answer system. The best example of this is a feature whereby once the applicant has inputted their postcode, the chatbot can then calculate how far they are from the nearest Anchor care home and then estimated commute times. The 'natural language' chatbot responses also ensured that the conversation retained a personal feel.

In less than a minute, the recruitment chatbot can:

- establish which role the candidate is interested in;
- see whether the location is within commutable distance;
- see whether the candidate has the required experience;
- capture multiple data points such as name, e-mail address and postcode.

Facebook Messenger is also becoming a platform for customer service, so it was important this was considered when building the chatbot. This resulted in building in functionality so that if the user had a specific question, they could be passed along to a member of the recruitment team while still on Messenger. The technology alone, however, was not enough to ensure success – the initiative involved building targeted social media campaigns that drove people to the chatbot where they could then apply.

The great things about Facebook ads for recruiting is that employers have data on everything: click-throughs, engagement, applications, etc. It allowed Anchor Trust to A/B test and optimize its messaging. Through analysing several months' worth of data, the firm was able to conclude what messages would appeal to its target audience the most. By delivering the right message to the right audience, the company was able to drive effective traffic to the chatbot to maximize applications.

In terms of lessons learned, Anchor Trust picked up some valuable insights from the process. The main consideration should be the development time for building a chatbot. Once the software has been built, there is a continuous process of analysing the data to see how it can be improved. If Anchor Trust was to create another chatbot, the HR team would allow for more time to test it before it goes live. There is always a risk with new technologies that it won't work as flawlessly as hoped, so you can never test too much. For example, over the course of the development of the chatbot, the company has learned that the language used is vital in guiding the applicant through the process and keeping them engaged. The HR team knows that emojis are popular online, so it incorporated them into the chatbot along with other informal language and GIF images to make the application process as fun and engaging as possible.

Simplifying the application process has significantly increased the number of applicants, while decreasing the cost per applicant. Data is king – continuously analysing results and data has allowed Anchor Trust to improve and evolve the chatbot to make the experience even better. Simply building a chatbot for interaction is not enough – employers must think about how people are going to discover it. They need an accompanying online advertising campaign to drive the people they want to apply onto the chatbot interface.

The launch of the tool has led to positive results and outcomes for the team. Since launching the chatbot, the company's HR team has attributed 86 hires directly to candidates who initiated contact with Anchor Trust through the bot. The 'traditional' recruitment method of applying for a job via uploading a CV to a website yielded a conversion rate of 2.04 per cent. The conversion rate for the chatbot stands at an unprecedented 27.35 per cent. The company performed 1,062 total chatbot conversations with potential applicants. All those who do not finish their application can be 'retargeted' via social campaigns to re-engage them. The average cost per applicant for previous recruitment campaigns was $68.55. The chatbot has reduced the cost per applicant by 64 per cent, and it now stands at $24.19. The number of average monthly applicants has increased 82 per cent overall.

Adapted from: HR Open Source[10]

Key points

- Due to the volume of applications relative to job openings, talent acquisition offers a wide variety of opportunities for automation through AI technologies from candidate screening to matching and more.

- One targeted application of machine learning technologies in recruiting is in reducing bias and improving diversity. In order to solve the bigger issues with diversity in the workplace we have to start with recruiting and move forward from there.

- Recruiting technology applications are incredibly varied and plentiful, serving niche use cases in almost any conceivable area. At the same time, larger players in the market are weaving in artificial intelligence to improve their own offerings to capture more market share.

Notes

1 https://www.ere.net/why-you-cant-get-a-job-recruiting-explained-by-the-numbers/

2 https://icoportal.s3.amazonaws.com/files/NHJgLCVQ/2017-Talent-Board-NAM-Research-Report-FINAL-180130.pdf

3 https://www.aeaweb.org/articles?id=10.1257/0002828042002561

4 https://www.sourcecon.com/human-vs-machine-who-sources-best-the-results-of-the-2017-grandmaster-competition/

5 https://www.shrm.org/hr-today/news/hr-magazine/0716/Pages/12-recruiting-tips-from-talent-acquisition-leaders.aspx

6 https://www.hrdive.com/news/salary-history-ban-states-list/516662/

7 http://www.businessinsider.com/unilever-artificial-intelligence-hiring-process-2017-6

8 https://www.tlnt.com/want-a-great-source-of-quality-hires-you-need-a-boomerang-program/

9 https://www.linkedin.com/pulse/year-our-recruiting-chatbot-anna-ott/

10 https://hros.co/case-study-upload/how-anchor-trust-leverages-chat-bots-to-drive-recruiting

Learning and development   06

Angel arrives at his tutoring session ready to dive in. The seven-year-old has been making progress on his subtraction with regrouping and is excited to see how well he can perform on the day's assignments. He spends some time initially in a small group setting, learning from a tutor with several other students near his level. After that, Angel moves on to computer games, honing his skills with practice. At the end of the day's session, he completes a short assessment to measure his progress before going home.

That same day, Maria is also scheduled to attend the tutoring session to help with her maths skills. She starts off with computer games and then moves to one-on-one time with an instructor. At the end of the day, she completes her own assessment to measure her progress.

Both of these students are in the same programme, but both of them receive different blends of instruction methods. Why? Because it's how they each learn best. This activity is part of the School of One, a project based in New York City and designed to help tailor teaching methods to each individual student. Unlike a normal classroom where every child receives more or less the same type of instruction, this programme gives students a highly personalized experience. The concept of individualized instruction is simple, even if the algorithm powering the learning delivery recommendations is fairly complex. Students receive a variety of instruction via some of the methods outlined above, and the regular assessments help to clarify which types of instruction are most suitable for each individual student. If Angel improves significantly on a day he has small group, the algorithm can recommend additional small group time in the next session to see if improvements continue to trend. Alternatively, if Maria is really doing well after computer games, the algorithm can pare back other types of delivery like one-on-one tutoring by weighting instructional delivery more heavily towards the methods that her brain prefers most. Excitingly, this gives teachers near real-time data on student performance and learning to help guide them toward mastery of skills on a repeatable basis.

This level of customization can be challenging to deliver, but the exciting outcome is that each individual participant is given the type of learning modality that best fits their need. What's interesting to consider is a more complex variant where Angel learns subtraction with regrouping best by computer game but needs one-on-one instruction to deal with fractions and small group time to focus on multiplication. In reality different topics may lend themselves to different learning methods in the same way that different learners may have their own unique set of preferences.

What does this have to do with today's business environment? As you may have guessed, the practical application of this type of adaptive learning has incredible implications not just on learning as a discipline, but on the outcomes of learning, such as engagement and/or performance. Plus, it's entirely enabled by a smart algorithm that continues refining as more data is introduced to the system on a regular basis. We as business leaders might be able to look for trends in the data and offer some customizations for certain learners, but there's no way we could do it individually for a large population. In one interview, Jesse Jackson pointed out that he wants to use technology to be more predictive in how learning paths and learning opportunities are offered to employees. This isn't based purely on what the employee likes or enjoys, but on the type of learning assets and experiences that will lead to the best performance and long-term career success. Jackson is the Chief Learning Officer for consumer and community banking at JPMorgan Chase, and he sees technology as a critical tool to support this transition from more transactional learning to high-impact learning that drives business results (Rio, 2018).[1] Jackson calls this the 'business of learning', and it is based on identifying the behaviours that lead to performance and developing tools to optimize performance to a higher level.

Let's take the discussion in a more 'meta' direction for a moment, because I need to touch on an area that's applicable across the business. Learning is at the heart of the adoption of artificial intelligence if for nothing more than the need for upskilling and reskilling the workforce to adapt to the changing technology landscape (Galagan, 2018).[2] Wal-Mart, the largest employer in the world, has invested more than US $2.7 billion to train its workforce on how to use newer technology offerings in addition to reskilling workers to better serve customers (Corkery, 2017).[3] While most of the headlines around the adoption of AI revolve around fear (AI will take all our jobs, robots are coming and the like), the truth is we don't yet know the full extent of the impact of AI adoption on the greater workforce. What we do know is that as technologies continue to come into play as I have highlighted throughout this book, L&D and talent development practitioners will have their hands full migrating the skills of workers to more broadly applicable capabilities. As Galagan points out in her writing, some areas might include helping learners manage their attention in an increasingly noisy digital workplace or helping steer workers towards future careers that are less susceptible to disruption by AI technologies. For more on this specific topic, in Chapter 9 I examine some of the key skills that talent leaders and the broader workforce should be cultivating in order to 'future proof' themselves in the age of AI and automation.

Another area I would expect to grow is helping workers to have more of an awareness of how artificial intelligence can augment their roles and how to best blend the human and machine components. How can we help our workforce to work alongside algorithms to improve performance, efficiency and results? I talk briefly about this concept of performance support technology later in this chapter. In essence I see it as a highly tailored version of the content of this book, delivered on a highly practical level to jobs and professions across the entire workforce. From the top executives to the early-career interns just getting into the business, learning professionals have the opportunity to help each group really understand AI technologies and how they might get the most out of leveraging them for their jobs. More importantly, it may even help to elevate the performance of those workers at the lower end of the performance scale. In an interview with a leader of a recruiting technology firm, the CEO explained that he sees artificial intelligence and machine learning as a way to

categorize and replicate the performance practices of the best workers, helping to distribute those competencies, behaviours and skills
into the rest of the workforce. By definition, that would mean that
your lower performers start to improve because they have the opportunity to mirror those practices used by their higher-performing
peers. Because L&D's reach and impact are stratified across the organization, the function can have a greater impact on the business
and its ability to react in an agile manner to this monumental shift.

Having a smart technology looking at the problem beyond the walls
of the learning department is important, because learning ultimately
isn't just a tool – it's a fundamental part of work itself. While formal
content may come from the learning team, informal learning takes place
every day as a part of the natural rhythm of work. Ultimately, learning
in a corporate context isn't just about cranking out more content or
more courses. That kind of quantity might have been the answer to a
problem in the past (unlikely, but I'm giving us the benefit of the doubt),
but today's learning leaders are more and more focused on quality content and learning assets as a way to enable better business performance.
It's not just to 'check the box' on delivering a set of training courses, it's
an opportunity to help each individual drive the organization's goals.
As one learning executive at McDonald's, Kevin M Yates, is fond of
saying, he's had business leaders come to him in the past with a problem
and a request for 'two live classes and a side of webinars' to resolve the
issue. In reality that may not address the problem, fix the problem, or
even be related to the problem. In those instances a deep level of curiosity is necessary to dig into the root of the issue and potential options to
solve it, whether that includes training or not.

In an interview with Chris Ponder, Head of Global HR Compliance
at Moneygram International, he shared a similar sentiment. All too
often training is seen as the solution to a problem when it may just
be treating a symptom of a larger issue. Managers constantly asking
questions about a process? Offering them training may fix the issue,
but it also might lead to poor decisions because the process is ultimately broken. An expert in performance improvement, Ponder believes that talent and learning leaders have to get better at practices
like the 'five why' concept, where the person trying to solve the
problem continues to ask 'why' until they reach the true root issue.

For instance: we have a problem with our learning content. Why? Because it's not improving our employees' performance. Why? Because learning content is requested by managers on an ad hoc basis. Why? Because we don't have a strong governance procedure to prioritize the right types of learning to meet our strategic goals. Aha! If we only stop at the first question where we have trouble with our learning content, we may try to change the modality, increase the amount of content, or something else. But by looking deeper we can ascertain the true cause of the problem and work to solve the real issue, not the surface-level problem that's easy to detect.

These are questions that humans are designed to solve, but that doesn't mean there is no place for AI technology in the learning realm. On the contrary, the applications are wide and varied, supporting everything from informal learning and collaboration to formal learning and content development. In terms of breaking down learning into specific areas of focus, that's a fairly logical way to do it. The widely-known 70-20-10 model, a staple of workplace learning theory, estimates that 10 per cent of learning at work happens from formal learning, 20 per cent from social experiences and collaboration and a whopping 70 per cent from experiential activities and the flow of work itself. For that reason we'll break down our analysis of AI applications and opportunities into formal and informal (social and experiential) applications. But first, let's consider what is perhaps the most high-impact area of AI application within the realm of L&D: the skills gap.

Closing the skills gap

A major area where AI can contribute to the learning function is by helping to minimize or even close the skills gap. Virtually every company would agree that they have some sort of skills gap in their organization. In one research study, my team found that the number one driver of learning content demand for employers was to close skills gaps (Lighthouse Research, 2017).[4] For purposes of a definition, the skills gap is the difference between the skills mix that their workers currently have and the skills mix the employer needs to accomplish its goals. That gap can be costly. A CareerBuilder study showed that the average cost of the skills gap to employers was around US $800,000 annually (2017).[5] The study looks at this from a recruiting perspective, because that's CareerBuilder's target market, but the concept isn't much different from what we would apply from a learning context. In the study, the $800,000 price tag includes everything from productivity loss and lower morale to higher turnover and revenue loss from the inability to hire the right people with the right skills to meet the needs of the employer.

How many of those companies could minimize or even solve their skills gap problems by leveraging training and development instead of trying to hire those individuals off the street? According to Josh Bersin's keynote presentation at the 2018 SkillSoft Perspectives event, it costs employers six times as much to hire for the skills they need as it does to develop them through training. If we combine this with data from the Wharton School, we see that external hires not only *cost more* money, but they also *perform worse* on average in their first two years on the job (Bidwell, 2011).[6] Between those two data points, it's astonishing that any employer prioritizes hiring over training to the degree that they do.

Now, here's where it gets really interesting. If we bring artificial intelligence into the conversation, imagine if the system was able to look at the job openings posted on the firm's applicant tracking system, highlight the critical skills gaps the firm is trying to hire for and start surfacing training for workers in those departments where the openings occurred or even across the enterprise. While the company is trying to find the right people through its recruiting efforts, the firm is also training its workers to flex their skills and grow their competencies to fill those gaps in the short term or even the longer term, if the positions are particularly difficult to recruit for. Another version of this could be searching the employee population for those with similar skills and abilities to the highest-performing individual that left the job and caused the vacancy to occur. For instance, it may be that someone working in a financial institution is more likely to be high-performing if they have previous experience in the insurance industry or within a technology firm, and the system can position those individuals as potential internal transfers that can be developed into the roles through internal mobility.

CASE STUDY   IHG combines assessments to quantify skills demand for diverse brands

IHG, a global hotel and leisure brand with nearly 400,000 global employees, leverages automated assessments during the hiring process to help weed out candidates that do not fit the personality characteristics of its multitude of diverse brands (Harrington, nd).[7] It also brings these tools to bear on reducing individual skills gaps.

Forget, for a moment, the wide spectrum of personality and skill needs within a single hotel. Front desk clerks, bell hops, cleaning staff, kitchen staff – set those groups aside for a moment. Now consider the fact that IHG has more than a dozen different hotel brands under its corporate umbrella. What constitutes performance success for someone in a Holiday Inn may be different for someone at a Kimpton Hotel, for instance. So how do you solve that?

The assessments IHG uses target the key personality traits that fit the needs of the specific hotel chain's brand, and then the company looks at skill availability as a measure of candidate quality. In the perfect world, candidates will be a culture or personality fit *and* a skills fit. But in reality, companies face decisions every day that have to do with picking a highly qualified person that doesn't fit the culture versus picking a person lacking in some key skills that really fits the culture well. In this example, maybe there are two candidates in the running for a specific opening. One of them has 10 years of experience managing a hotel but doesn't quite fit the personality and cultural characteristics of the hotel brand they have applied to work for. The other person only has two years of hotel management experience, but it was in a substantially similar hotel and they have the right attitude and values. Both are qualified in their own way, so how do we select the right person?

IHG has committed itself to filtering out those poor-fit candidates and dedicating its learning and development resources to training for the right skills to get other candidates into shape. Again, while there may be a core type of training that each brand needs to establish a base level of skills in candidates, each of the 13 different brands has its own performance standards and expectations for workers. This complex need is one that is best suited to applications of artificial intelligence.

Formal learning applications for AI

Formal learning is what most of our time, effort and resources go to as learning leaders. After all, formal learning encompasses eLearning, instructor-led content and more. These formal activities also include content. Lots and lots of content. For perspective, PwC has approximately 1 million pieces of learning content in its library. The sheer volume of content the company has generated is hard to wrap my mind around, but times are changing. In the past it was enough for learning teams to produce or purchase volumes of content and present it to the learner. Mission accomplished. Today, though, times have changed. More than ever learners are circumventing the learning management system (LMS) in favour of Google or other preferred sources of information. Additionally, our research at Lighthouse shows that low-performing companies are seven times more likely to say their learning content doesn't engage learners or is highly transactional. Great content helps to create an engaging experience for learners. In an interview with one global L&D leader, he explained that this increasing trend of focusing on 'experiences' was borderline rubbish. When pressed, he explained that no learning executive would get budget for technology or resources merely to make learning prettier or more engaging for the sake of it. However, if the outcome of creating a more engaging experience was that learners retained more information, were more likely to change behaviours, or were more likely to improve performance, then businesses would be much more willing to invest in the concept of learning experience design. This jives with another finding in that same research, showing that high-performing companies are 50 per cent more likely to say that engaging learning content helps to enable consumption of critical learning resources. Simply put – learning experiences matter.

One way to measure learning experiences is by examining adoption rates of learning content. Voluntary consumption would indicate more engaging content and experiences, but as you can see in Figure 6.1, many companies do not use this practice regularly. High-performing firms are about 10 times more likely to look at adoption rates to measure the impact of learning content, and they are more likely to measure every facet of learning than low performers (Lighthouse Research, 2017).[8]

Figure 6.1 Creating engaging learning experiences

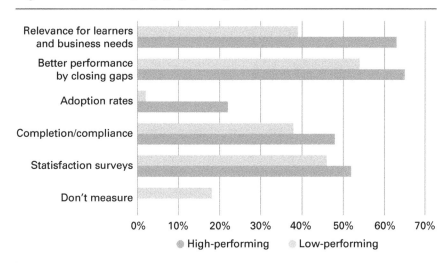

SOURCE 2017 Learning Content Strategy Study, Lighthouse Research & Advisory (n = 152)

One type of learning content that employers have and will continue to rely on is instructor-led training. A variety of research points to instructor-led training as the most commonly used and most effective method of instructing workers, so we'll start there. Instructor-led training, or ILT, is the most familiar type of learning process for us. We've received years of schooling and this is often the default method employers use for sharing information and training throughout the organization. While artificial intelligence probably won't be taking the place of the trainer at the front of the room any time soon, there are roles that AI can play that will improve the efficiency of ILT.

One firm, Training Orchestra, offers a technology that supports employers' need to manage the various disparate resources connected to offering live training. Think about the logistics of planning a training class: you need an instructor, a space, a way to track registration, materials, presentation tools, attendees and more. It's no surprise then that most employers don't make efficient use of those resources. Your top trainers and most sought-after training spaces might be leveraged heavily, but there's almost always room for optimization and improvement. Training Orchestra manages more than US $5 billion in training investments across its client base, helping customers to get the most out of their resources by helping with scheduling, planning, and resource allocation.

AI embedded in this type of technology would offer some incredible benefits. For instance, classes with open slots for attendees might be flagged and prioritized so trainers and managers know where to send available workers. Or maybe the AI sees that there's a consistent no-show rate of 10 per cent for one of the trainers, so it overbooks classes by 5–10 per cent to help avoid lost opportunities. Another option? The AI realizes a class is not going to be full so it can move it to a smaller room to save the larger space for other activities, automatically notifying participants about the change. Again, ILT is a major portion of the average learning budget. According to Stéphane Pineau, CEO of Training Orchestra, formal training makes up 65 per cent of the average learning budget but employers don't do a great job of making sure they get the most out of their systems and processes.[9] Companies that partner with the firm see an average of 20 per cent optimization the first year and incremental changes after that. While your next course probably won't be taught by a robotic instructor, there is clearly a valid opportunity for AI to support the process.

For many years, the default piece of technology companies have bought to support their L&D needs has been a learning management system. The purpose of the tool is to deliver content and track completion rates, but not much else, which is why my firm has seen an explosion of learning experience platforms in the market in recent years. In a recent discussion with the visionary CEO of Docebo, a learning technology firm headquartered in Toronto, we discussed the concept of a fully automated learning system. Claudio Erba started Docebo in 2005 and since then has led the market with a variety of innovations, from incorporating informal learning components into the system to looking at AI elements that can radically change the expectations for administrators and learners. His belief is that we should start with the highly transactional processes administrators have to manage, such as learner enrolments, for automation. Unlike some who want to focus on the automation from the learner end, Erba wants to focus hard on automating and augmenting the capabilities of L&D professionals to make their lives easier and enable them to focus on more strategic activities.

CASE STUDY   AI enables teaching at scale

Teaching is greatly enhanced by creating personal connections with students. But how can instructors of college courses with hundreds of students create a more personalized experience? For instance, in just one online Georgia Tech class, students interact with teachers, teaching assistants and each other through online forums. However, the volume of interaction is staggering. Just one virtual class in the computer science department can have up to 350 students per semester, and discussion forums are incredibly active. To help professors manage the workload, the university has authorized the use of teaching assistants to support the demand. One of those assistants who had recently started working with students was Jill Watson. Jill was conscientious, diligent and always courteous in her responses to student requests. In fact, she was such a great help that the professor actually nominated her for teaching assistant of the year out of appreciation for her efforts. He said he was very interested in seeing how the university handled Jill's nomination, since this was the first time a non-human had been nominated in the history of the programme. Yes, Jill was a bot! And, as you may have guessed, she was incredibly effective at her job. But it didn't start out that way. The story below tells of her conception, issues and triumphant finish (Lipko, 2016).[10]

During one semester, those 350 students per class post an average of 10,000 messages. That's essentially the same as receiving 100 e-mails a day for 100 days, and the university estimates it would require employing an instructor full-time for a year to respond to all those messages individually. This caused the course instructor, Ashok Goel, to wonder if AI could be used to answer the most frequently asked questions. Since new student cohorts ask virtually the same questions over and over again, the hope was an AI assistant might help to alleviate the strain of responding to thousands of messages and free teaching staff to focus on more creative aspects of the course, including more nuanced discussions.

Goel and his team began by giving the AI assistant, named Jill Watson to disguise its identity as a bot, a consolidated memory of all question and answer pairs from previous semesters. Then they organized the information into categories based on the types of questions asked. During testing, the team would ask a question and Jill would have to search previous pairings of questions and answers for a suitable response.

In January 2016, the professor introduced Jill Watson as one of his new teaching assistants and students did not know that this was an automated bot. Like any new teaching assistant, the system offered responses that were sometimes right and sometimes wrong or strange. For example, a student asked a technical question about computer languages to use in a project, and the response from Jill focused on assignment length for a research paper. Goel said it was much like raising a child, requiring constant support and direction. To help avoid erroneous support and feedback, the team created a mirror forum, allowing Jill to answer questions in a simulated environment hidden from students. If the response was good, a human teaching assistant approved the message. If not, it was not posted. Over time, performance improved incrementally, and when accuracy reached 97 per cent for Jill's responses the bot was returned to the live discussion board environment among the 350 students.

One of the most appealing value points for the system was responsiveness. A student in Shanghai could get a response as fast as a student in London or the Middle East. Jill enabled responsiveness 24 hours a day, seven days a week, and 365 days a year. Goel's team actually had to code a time delay into Jill's responses so students would not suspect the system was artificially intelligent. Later in the semester, a curious student finally wondered via the forum if Jill was an AI or not, and Goel came clean about the experiment. Today, all teaching assistants for his courses are using pseudonyms and Jill's name is masked so new students don't know which is the bot and which is a real human. The long-term questions Goel is curious about answering are whether AI really does reduce teaching staff load, whether it encourages knowledge retention, or if it impacts student engagement to a measurable degree, but it's too early to tell at this stage.

Learning content and curation

Let's shift gears a bit to content. I've said for quite some time that curation is the new creation for L&D professionals, meaning that learning leaders need to get comfortable with helping to curate and find great resources instead of trying to justify their value purely through the creation of new learning objects. With workers having the option to search online for virtually any resource, they have less pressure to visit the employer's learning management system to find learning content and assets. That change in pressure is a good thing, but it also shifts what the employer needs from its L&D team. Instead of feeling like they need to create learning content for every eventuality and every unique need, learning teams can prioritize development of specialized content that they can't buy or find off the shelf elsewhere. Additionally, they can put more effort into curating the best experiences for learners to ensure that content drives engagement and higher-level learning outcomes. As you might imagine, that curation component can be augmented with artificial intelligence. Here are a few examples of how that might work.

Historically the only way for learning teams to find out what people need is to wait for a request. And by then there's already a need and therefore designing, creating and launching the content means the need may have changed or disappeared entirely by the time the learning team can respond. But what if there was an advance mechanism to see what people need before they ask for it outright? One signal for this would be search volume. Companies could use an algorithm to capture and record common searches in the learning management system, company knowledgebase or intranet. If employees are consistently looking for content around a specific topic and it doesn't exist, that can spur a discussion about whether that content needs to be developed. Alternatively, if content already exists on those commonly searched topics, the firm can curate the best resources focused on answering those questions and feature them in a more prominent location, so employees don't have to work as hard to find them.

It's no stretch to believe that artificial intelligence should be able to do this automated curation without human input. When it comes down to it, people may not even ask for help with something they need to do their job. I've seen in the past highly qualified individuals who were hired for a high-profile role, and then were tentative about asking for help and appearing like they were not fit for the job. It's one of those quirky human traits that is hard to predict from person to person and company to company, because some cultures are more supportive of collaboration than others. Additionally, barriers to this scenario may exist because people don't want to appear incompetent or unprepared for the job, or it may simply be that they don't know the right question to ask of a peer or manager. However, all of us have been trained with the availability of search engines to instinctively search for information we need.

Another example of machine learning speeding up the learning curve is by surfacing content that is relevant to you. Not to your peers. Not to your boss. But to you. Because the learning system knows your job, your history of completed training, your performance records, your informal consumption of learning content (more on this in the 'informal' section below) and your career aspirations, it can serve up content automatically that helps you to close critical skills gaps and move you towards your ultimate goals. Instead of getting a generic piece of content when you log into the system, it offers to let you pick up where you left off, take a course based on the next career role you want to take, or strengthen a competency that you've always struggled with. The idea that your learning system knows you that well is intriguing, but imagine that scaling across a company of 100,000 people. Every single one of them is receiving targeted, personalized learning experiences that have been curated to meet their specific needs.

In addition, any opportunity to upskill workers and improve their capabilities is a win, so leveraging a bot could offer another option. We've seen throughout this book that bots offer a variety of opportunities to support personalized interactions with workers at scale. One solution in the market today is Sunlight. Sunlight is a new learning platform that gives employees ownership over their own professional development. Employers can actually offer this kind of self-directed learning option as an employee benefit, because a wide base of research shows that workers are heavily driven by the desire to grow and develop. Sunlight accomplishes this by helping employers give each worker their own learning budget to spend as they see fit. Sunlight has a marketplace of resources and learning assets to select from, but as we've already discussed, the sheer amount of content can be overwhelming. That's where the chatbot comes in. Sunlight's chatbot offers a concierge experience, so workers can converse with the system to home in on resources, content and assets that can help them to achieve their learning and career goals. Most employers couldn't dedicate the budget to hire an individual simply to serve in this 'learning concierge' role, but a bot can accomplish it by carrying out discussions with as many workers as needed around the world at any time.

With more and more learning happening in the moment and being driven by learner exploration, some say that formal learning is going to take a back seat to informal learning in the workplace. However, I always say that nobody ever learned to be a doctor by watching YouTube. There will always be a need for formal learning to help guide employees, managers and executives to the right learning and performance outcomes.

Informal learning applications for AI

Humans are self-developing, self-directed and self-interested. This set of points forms the core of a talk I give around the myths and truths of informal learning. In recent years I've witnessed a resurgence of interest in the concept of informal learning, and employers seem to be very interested in how to not only establish environments where this happens more freely, but also environments where they can track the impact and results of informal learning. An exploration of each of those three points explains the biological imperative to learn and grow as a human being.

For instance, we are self-developing. We are natural explorers. I make this point pretty clearly later in the book when I talk about the skills to future-proof yourself in a more automated workplace. The curiosity component drives us to ask questions and explore ideas, sometimes beyond what is even considered rational. We observe, form a hypothesis, experiment, reach a conclusion and then repeat as necessary. I always use the joke that this doesn't happen consciously: when the first caveman saw his neighbour eaten by a sabre-toothed tiger, he didn't verbally hypothesize that he shouldn't go outside at night to avoid being eaten himself.

Additionally, we are self-directed. Each of us has a different brain in a very physical sense. When you learn the history about the capital of India or how to perform a process in your job better, you store that information in a different place than I would, even if we both consumed the exact same type of learning content. That's because our brains find ways to connect the concepts to other information already stored in our brains so that it is better retained. Maybe you have visited India so your brain finds ways to make those connections while you learn about it, but mine instead makes connections to a news story I read about it in the past. Because our brains process information differently, we can't expect all learners to learn the same way.

Finally, we are self-interested. Simply put, we don't pay attention to boring things. Think for a second: *exactly* how many seconds did it take you to put on your shoes this morning? If you're like me, you might not even remember the exact moment when you did. That's because your brain eliminates or marginalizes any information it deems irrelevant. The impact on learning is pretty clear. Do the learning moments you are creating for your learners rise to the level where our brains will actually pay attention?

These three components explain the 'why' behind informal learning, but the biggest challenge of informal learning is how to capture it. As long as people have been alive they have been using components of both social and experiential learning. When my three-year-old son learned to unlock my phone and turn on the drawing application, there was no formal course. I didn't offer an assessment and an instructor-led lecture on the proper methods and ethics of unlocking smartphones. He simply watched and repeated the action. In this case I can observe the outcome of the action, but it's not always so clear-cut in the workplace. Smart technologies like artificial intelligence can help with this issue of tracking and categorizing information that we learn in the flow of work. For example, what if the learning system plugged into the collaboration tools employers use? For example, employers may have Slack, Microsoft Teams, or other systems to capture ongoing conversations and enable collaboration among employees. How much informal learning happens among those employees on a daily basis that could be captured as knowledge? If the bot consumes all of the questions and answers, it may be able to present answers back before a human could see the message and respond. For instance, if James asks Mary how to complete a procedure and she gives him the response, the next time Alex asks

Mary how to complete the same procedure the system could answer on her behalf, speeding up the transfer of knowledge and saving Mary's time for something else more valuable. This is similar to the concept of Georgia Tech incorporating a bot into classroom forums to support student questions.

Several years ago I worked with an L&D leader from MasterCard to share the company's success story of adopting a new learning methodology. A core component of the transition was regular video collaboration among the workers, because it isn't always cost-effective to bring learners together into one place for regularly scheduled sessions. But the challenge with video, even two-way video with participants, is engagement. When training someone in a classroom, we can tell if they are engaged, collaborative, interactive and so on. In a virtual environment it can be more challenging to understand those dynamics. One company that's trying to sort through this is onQ. Active learning is more engaging than passive learning and that's one of the core challenges of using video as a medium – learners are passive. onQ addresses this by scoring engagement, sentiment, facilitation and other outcomes. Imagine being able to analyse an audience of learners consuming video content to be able to tell what their general sentiment and engagement was for the duration of the session? As a trainer and speaker, I would love to have those kinds of analytics to understand which parts of my presentations resonate with the audience and which don't in order to continuously improve the content, delivery and tone.

Learning has always placed some prioritization on the content itself, but in recent years this focus has shifted from an employer-designed repository of information that employees can visit to a more personalized, employee-driven experience. Workers now have the opportunity to seek out their own learning content and have their learning technology follow them and record that consumption outside the walls of the learning management system. For instance, learning experience platforms like Degreed and ContentSphere are set up to capture learning activities on a broader scale. Read an article about an industry trend? Watch a TED talk to improve your leadership skills? Those types of activities are tracked and recorded in the system, offering a more complete picture of your learning.

Every company knows that learning isn't about completing courses – it's about gathering skills and improving performance. Employers are using these learning experience platforms to help manage employee learning not in the traditional sense, but by giving employees the ability to capture their learning activities on a broader scale (Read an article? Watched a video? It's all in your profile). These tools give L&D leaders a leg up on that challenge. What truly excites me about these kinds of technologies are their attempts to focus on outcomes like talent mobility or employee growth versus just counting the number of courses or articles someone consumes as a measure of success. Too often learning sees quantity of content delivered as its measure of success, when in reality it should be the improvement of the people and the organization.

Coaching and mentoring

How about coaching? In our study of what separates high-performing companies from others when it comes to performance management practices, the top performers are more likely to use performance coaching as a key component of their talent practices. This is often used for line-level workers, but managers are sometimes forgotten about in the shuffle. Two of the tools in the marketplace today that help solve this problem are dedicated solutions like Butterfly.ai and components of larger systems like Leadership Actions in Ultimate Software's UltiPro system. The core component of both systems is a qualitative analysis of employee qualitative comments such as surveys and prior performance review data. By crunching those inputs the system can generate recommendations personalized to the managers about how to improve their leadership style, performance and results.

This concept of a 'robot coach' includes the positive aspects of coaching: an informal, supportive and continuous conversation about how to improve results. Additionally, because the system can see actual performance record data, it may be able to give even more accurate coaching than a human intermediary. And, similar to the adaptive learning concept explored in the School of One example that opened this chapter, these systems should theoretically be able to see ongoing performance and employee feedback data to understand if interventions have been successful at changing behaviour or not. Finally, any trends in the skill gaps of leaders could be tracked and funnelled to learning teams in order to develop or curate more targeted resources. For example, if workers are consistently complaining about leadership shortfalls in communications, tools and strategies can be shared with the management team in a more holistic manner to address the widespread issue.

Performance support

One of the last components we'll look at in the learning realm is performance support. A few things set performance support apart from other training types: it is accessible at the point/moment of need, embedded into the flow of work, and helps solve a specific problem. I love the concept of performance support because it supports a very pure definition of learning: it's not about the content or the company, it's about improving performance. One company that's really bringing AI components into performance support is Axonify. The firm's system helps employers to codify and replicate best practices on the job. One retail client saw more than 16,000 per cent return on investment after it started using the technology. The core idea is that contextual information in the flow of work is going to be a game-changer for performance, quality and so much more. Think about one of the best performers you've ever worked with, whether in the office or outside of it. What did that person do differently from others that set them apart in terms of performance? Was it a specific habit? A communication method? A situational awareness? Whatever it might be, performance support systems will have the capability to capture those differentiators for the best performers and help to replicate them for the rest of us with contextual alerts, timely recommendations and guided help.

Looking forward: virtual, augmented and mixed reality technologies

To this point I have avoided talking about the increasing adoption of virtual reality (VR), augmented reality (AR) and mixed reality (MR) technologies. It's not because I believe them to be unimportant; I just believe their most valuable contributions will most likely come in the form of training. One of my earliest career experiences as an HR professional involved working for a firm that creates simulation software for military radios, helicopter pilots and students studying aviation in college. From those early days I was able to see not only how the technologies were developed, but also how they actually improved performance for learners. We know that practice and application are some of the best ways to cement learning and help workers demonstrate their newly learned skills and knowledge, and for some professions this is more easily done with simulated environments that virtual and augmented reality offer. Several years ago I published a case study of HP's augmented reality printer support tool. Users could focus a smartphone or tablet camera on a specific printer and the application would render a three-dimensional animation overlay on the printer, demonstrating how to change ink cartridges in real time. This is a simplistic example, but imagine doing this for physicians with a surgical procedure, maintenance technicians on a routine service process and so on.

On the virtual reality front, several firms have entered the market with virtual reality training tools that are claiming very high learning retention compared to more traditional, passive training methods. Because of the rise of the #MeToo movement, one area of focus for virtual reality content has been sexual harassment training. This is the confluence of several components. For instance, the findings by the Equal Employment Opportunity Commission that traditional sexual harassment training doesn't work helped to shock the industry into more comprehensive thinking around training for behaviour modification, not just to passively share information (Folz, 2016).[11] Additionally, as mentioned earlier in this chapter, there's an incredible need to train workers in more progressive ways to capture their attention and ensure relevance and retention of the information being presented.

Learning, as we've seen here, has much to gain from the advent and incorporation of new AI technologies. From simplifying the life of the administrator to delivering better learner experiences, the sky is the limit for what we can expect to see as the learning profession embraces automation and machine learning-based systems.

Key points

- Because every learner is different, companies often struggle to offer the right content and medium that makes sense for everyone. AI technologies can help to identify the best methods on an individual level, improving learning outcomes.

- A significant portion of learning happens not in a classroom, but through informal learning and collaboration. Artificial intelligence can help not only to match up learners and mentors but also to capture those informal learning moments in ways traditional technologies can't.

- Looking forward, a blend of AR, VR and MR will help to create more life-like learning scenarios and situations to drive active learning. Unlike passive consumption of learning content, trainers can generate visceral reactions that solidify learning concepts far beyond the walls of the classroom.

Notes

1 http://www.clomedia.com/2018/03/19/jesse-jackson-accidental-clo-intentional-learning/

2 https://www.td.org/td-magazine/may-2018-td-magazine-measurement-and-evaluation-issue

3 https://www.nytimes.com/2017/08/08/business/walmart-academy-employee-training.html

4 http://lhra.io/blog/new-research-radically-rethinking-learning-content-strategy-free-report/

5 http://press.careerbuilder.com/2017-04-13-The-Skills-Gap-is-Costing-Companies-Nearly-1-Million-Annually-According-to-New-CareerBuilder-Survey

6 https://faculty.wharton.upenn.edu/wp-content/uploads/2012/03/
Paying_More_ASQ_edits_FINAL.pdf

7 https://www.thepeoplespace.com/practice/articles/how-international-
hotel-giant-ihg-using-artificial-intelligence-bring-hr-and

8 http://lhra.io/blog/new-research-radically-rethinking-learning-content-
strategy-free-report/

9 https://trainingorchestra.com/collaborative-learning-ecosystem-
explained/

10 https://pe.gatech.edu/blog/meet-jill-watson-georgia-techs-first-ai-
teaching-assistant

11 https://www.shrm.org/hr-today/news/hr-news/pages/eeoc-harassment-
task-force.aspx

Talent management

In my teen years I was given the task of repairing a piece of our workshop's roof that had been damaged by a storm. I was excited about the opportunity, because I am probably the least handy person you will find. If you had to pick a team to build a table or assemble a bookshelf, I'd be the last one chosen (if anyone picked me at all!). Yet here I had the opportunity to fix something and prove my worth. To be honest, I was incredibly excited. I would finally undo the years of being 'unhandy' and show off my dormant skills.

I gathered the tools, purchased the material to cover the hole, and drove over to the building. Upon arrival, I realized a critical error on my part. The ladder would not reach the roof. I looked around the workshop but could not find a place low enough to climb up, so I opened the roll-up door and drove inside. Bingo! I realized that if I backed up the truck against the wall, I could put the ladder in the truck bed and climb out onto the roof. I scrambled up the ladder, materials in hand. Once I reached the top of the building and got settled, I went to work. In just a few short minutes, I had repaired the problem, and while it wasn't as good as new, it certainly didn't have a gaping hole anymore. I took a few minutes to soak in the glory, enjoying the beautiful view of the countryside beside me. And then I realized my mistake.

Remember, I had climbed onto the roof *through* that hole. The one that I had just patched closed. I was left with no apparent way to get down. I debated every option I could think through. Should I hang off the side and drop, potentially breaking my ankle or leg? Could I call someone to bring me a longer ladder to get down? Maybe I could remove the repairs I had just made to climb back down the ladder and return later? After some thought, I took one last look around the edges of the roof's perimeter. As luck would have it, one corner had a small section of roof that extended out about halfway between the roofline and the ground, which allowed me to ultimately climb down safely, but this story parallels the conversation we're having around technology in an interesting way. In this example, I created an entirely new problem (being trapped) by solving an old one (fixing the roof). The world of AI is not dissimilar. When it solves one problem another may arise. For example, creating an algorithm to manage worker scheduling, payments and feedback seems like a great way to level the playing field, reduce bias and improve worker engagement. After all, we've always heard that 'people leave managers, not companies', so pulling the manager out of the process seems like a step in the right direction. But is that type of work environment really as great as it sounds? Consider this example of Uber's algorithm for managing workers.

Replacing humans with algorithms: hard lessons learned

Uber, one of the most well-known companies in the world, has become the de facto standard for explaining the gig economy, how it operates and its broader impact on the marketplace. The simplicity of being able to push a button on your phone and have a vehicle show up to drive you anywhere you want to go within minutes truly is an impressive service. The company has a brilliant slogan for those interested in joining as drivers: be your own boss. In every advertisement seeking drivers for the company, the messages are positive and seem to indicate that drivers have control over their environment, assignments and schedule. After all, while it has been a heated debate thus far, Uber's assertion that drivers are independent contractors, not employees, has continued to define the nature of the relationship. For reference, a few key components for independent contractors that differentiate them from employees are the options to choose what clients they want to serve, what hours they want to work and what rate of pay they want to accept. With more people seeking flexibility and additional income opportunities, Uber seems to offer a solution that allows workers to turn the app on when they want to work and off when they don't – the ultimate in flexible work opportunities.

Yet it's not perfect. Drivers are managed by a faceless algorithm that tracks their every move, and they often feel coerced into taking drives even if they don't want to. But it goes deeper than that. Drivers have found that they receive different rates of commissions and have different bonus targets assigned with no insight into how the numbers are calculated. In addition, some drivers feel like they are being denied opportunities to drive when they are close to reaching bonus thresholds (Solman, 2017).[1] This lack of transparency seems to be at odds with the claim that drivers are independent contractors, but this isn't the forum to debate the idea. Instead, let's look at this idea of being managed by an algorithm and how that affects the very human drivers at the other end of the employment relationship. A study was performed that examined how drivers are fighting back against the algorithm in an attempt to regain some sense of their humanity and control. Drivers use a handful of options, including switching to other ride-sharing apps or even switching off the app at critical times, to make their point. According to Paul Hebert, an expert on motivation and influence in the workplace, this is called 'negative reciprocity'.[2] Negative reciprocity occurs when individuals act out against unfavourable treatment in an effort to balance the scales within a system. Hebert explained that this often happens in less extreme ways in other workplaces, such as when employers have overly strict dress codes. Employees are always looking for a way to keep the power from shifting too much towards the employer and will take actions both large and small to keep things in check.

Take UberPOOL, for example. Unlike the original UberX offering, which allows a person to take a private ride to their destination, UberPOOL rides are cheap because they are supposed to allow drivers to pick up multiple passengers on the same route. While it sounds good in theory, UberPOOL payouts for drivers are lower than the already inexpensive rates for normal rides, and it adds layers of logistical complexity that can challenge drivers. For example, if my driver stops to pick up two more people after picking me up, I might rate the driver poorly for a slow trip even though she doesn't have the option of not picking up the other riders. Consistent low ratings can hamper the driver's ability to get future ride assignments. For these and other reasons, drivers typically try to avoid answering UberPOOL requests, but they can be punished for failing to accept rides that Uber assigns for them. One workaround that some drivers have found is to accept the first rider on UberPOOL trips and then ignore other requests until the trip is complete, allowing them to pocket the normal UberX commission instead of the lower UberPOOL commission.

Additionally, drivers have taken to online forums and social media sites to organize themselves and find more effective ways to protect their interests. For instance, drivers will organize mass switch-offs of the driving application to trigger surge pricing. In areas where there are more riders than drivers, surge pricing kicks in to balance the supply and demand of resources. When drivers switch off and re-move the supply, rider demand can trigger surge pricing. Once trig-gered, drivers can switch their apps back on by communicating with each other on back channels and take advantage of the new, higher prices and corresponding higher payouts for drivers.

At the same time, if any issue that arises, such as emergency situa-tions with passengers or simple technical issues with the app, drivers have a very challenging time communicating with an actual person at Uber for support. NPR did a study with nearly 1,000 Uber drivers to understand their issues and challenges, finding that nearly eight out of ten drivers were unable to speak with a human when they needed help from the company (Shahani, 2017).[3] Imagine having an issue at work, whether emergency-related or simply process-related in your daily routine. Now imagine not being able to ask anyone, not even a single person, about how to solve the issue. That's a hint of the reality these individuals face when they sign up as drivers.

This story is incredibly relevant to this concept of talent manage-ment, because as time progresses I expect to see more companies hoping to insert algorithms and bots into the management relation-ship for employees. From helping to give recognition for a job well done to reviewing performance scores to providing insight on future career and succession opportunities, there are a wide variety of use cases for adopting artificial intelligence technology in the talent management arena. While there are ways to do that strategically, this provides a cautionary tale for what it looks like when employers go too far to the side of automation. At the end of the day, people want to be managed by people. There are 'self-serve' options for reviewing your own goals, looking at potential career paths, and so on, but we have a fundamental need to connect with others. Hebert's reaction to this story was that we need better human managers, not better HR technology. I think the right answer is a blend of the two. We need better ways to train our managers, and some of those were covered in the previous chapter, but we also need better technology to help managers understand how to support their people in a variety of situations, from growing their career to enabling their performance and beyond.

The critical role of managers in talent management

As the example from Uber shows, managing workers is a fundamentally human activity. There are opportunities for AI to take over some of the more mundane or laborious aspects of the job, such as setting worker schedules, but the activities like giving feedback, encouraging performance and discussing career opportunities and growth aren't something we can just hand over to an algorithm. The typical definition of talent management from a process and technology standpoint encompasses areas like performance management, succession and career pathing. However, we're also going to bring in engagement and recognition systems as well since they are inherently tied to that incredibly valuable manager–employee relationship. How valuable? Managers account for up to 70 per cent of variance in employee engagement scores (Beck and Harter, 2015).[4] In nearly any area of the business, if there is a single point of failure that is responsible for a 70 per cent swing in results, employers would be finding ways to add backup systems or spread the risk, yet for some reason managers are not treated the same way. That's one reason I'm particularly excited to see AI technologies come to this area of HR. Managing others is a tough job. I get it. And yet businesses still operate arcane manager selection practices such as 'this person is a great performer, so let's make them a manager over other employees'. This type of approach often has disastrous results, yet it's still incredibly common.

In the book *All In: How the best managers create a culture of belief and drive big results* (Free Press, 2012), authors Elton and Gostick talk about an experiment at a large organization where teams with good performance were categorized as green and those with poor performance were categorized as red. The organization then swapped managers from the teams so that red teams got a green manager and green teams got a red manager. Within a few months the green managers had elevated the performance of the red team to green while the red managers had diminished the performance of the green teams to red. What this reinforces is just how heavily managers can influence team performance. We know this anecdotally when we work for good or not-so-good managers, but there is a variety of data to support the idea that managers matter to a great extent in the employment relationship. As in the Uber example, there is a place on the spectrum of automation that goes too far in taking the humanity out of the process, but the average company today has a lot of space to run if they want to introduce automation and stretch the capabilities of their managers.

One story I've been very interested in following focuses on who gives recognition within organizations. O C Tanner did an analysis of employers and found that the givers of recognition matter just as much as the receivers (Beckstrand, Rogers and Sturt, 2016).[5] One of the interesting findings in the study was that non-managers give fewer recognitions overall, but those that do participate actually give more frequently than managers themselves. When I'm in a group of HR leaders and we are talking about working with our management staff, one of the inevitable issues is that managers aren't great at giving recognition or feedback to employees. What this study shows is that some non-managers may already have that competency built in, which would potentially be a signal for moving them into a managerial role at some point. After all, if these individual contributors are already predisposed to offering recognition to their peers, why not harness that in a managerial role? What's exciting to consider is how we could leverage AI tools for analysing how recognition flows in and among the workforce. For example, if the system sees an individual that is consistently recognizing peers and others for their work efforts, it might also scan the person's own performance records to see if they should be flagged as a management candidate for succession purposes. While it seems like a relatively simple process, it surely beats the common management selection practices of choosing the person with the most tenure, picking the individual that wants the job (even if it's not a good fit), or moving the best performer into the position and taking away the job in which they were performing well.

Employee engagement

Employee engagement is about more than moving some score up or down by a few points with a survey. I'm convinced that employers have become 'engagement weary' in the last few years, because despite spending in a variety of areas little has changed with engagement. One of the main issues I speak about when I'm discussing this with business executives is the need to go beyond engagement to look at actual business metrics and outcomes. There are a variety of research studies correlating employee engagement levels with things like innovation, safety, quality, revenue, shareholder value, customer satisfaction, retention and so on. Those are the metrics we need to be talking about when we discuss engagement, especially if we want leaders to buy in and support this idea.

An opportunity for AI to support this would be to pull those disparate measures into a dashboard and show as close to real time as possible which were correlated in a particular business and to what extent. For example, a healthcare firm might see correlations between engagement and quality more strongly than a financial services firm. Or, if the connections are there, they may be stronger in one firm or another because of size, industry or culture. AI would be ideally suited to examining these connections and correlations to define the relationships at a firm and how they adjust over time based on changes in engagement levels. What excites me about this is that engagement could be seen as a leading indicator for key business metrics. While HR leaders are typically not experts in statistical correlation and analysis, an algorithm could easily make these connections and then use predictions to show 'what if' analyses based on changes in engagement. For example, if engagement increases by three points, the employer might be able to expect a 5 per cent rise in sales or a 2 per cent bump in customer satisfaction scores.

To take it a step further, the system could also work on the other end of the spectrum to help drive up engagement in meaningful ways. Because we know managers play a significant role in engagement variance, the system could suggest ways managers could improve communications and engagement levels. For instance, in a conversation with one technology firm that offers both performance management and learning management technologies, the product team saw retention data was connected with managers who held regular one-on-one discussions with their team members. The more likely managers were to have these meetings with their team members, the more likely those team members were to stay. Additionally, a discussion with an HR executive at a large aerospace firm shed some light on the company's findings around manager and employee relations. The team found that managers with larger teams were much more likely to have issues with engagement and worker satisfaction, which is a logical conclusion. A manager with three employees should be able to connect more deeply with the team than a manager with 10 employees. If we combine those two data points, it demonstrates an opportunity for AI to help guide managers towards more meaningful relationships. Some of the simpler AI applications like smart notifications could help managers to ensure they stay on top of regular discussions with their team members. However, more in-depth tools might give managers insights into which team members might present a flight risk based on a wide variety of signals and behaviours. These kinds of insights are most helpful when accompanied by prescriptive insights and ideas that can help managers know how to take the next steps to improve the relationship. Engagement, from a practical standpoint, is about helping workers to feel like they are appreciated enough that they give their full effort at work. Algorithms can't make that happen without human intervention, but by enabling managers to have better insights, information and notifications the systems can guide them towards better relationships with their team members.

One of the key issues with engagement is that it's often measured by a survey. While there's nothing inherently wrong with surveys, they don't always offer a full picture of the issues that employees are dealing with on a daily basis. AI tools enable companies to take a deeper dive into survey data with sentiment analysis technology. I touched on the broader implications of sentiment analysis in Chapter 3, but one of the clear use cases is around employee engagement. An example of a firm making use of deeper types of employee data is Community Bridges. The non-profit organization employs 1,500 people and is based in Arizona. Maddie Nichols, Chief Human Resources Officer, said the firm has been doing standard surveys for quite some time to understand employee needs and issues at work (Ultimate Software, 2018).[6] As a provider of care services for individuals battling substance abuse, it's easy to imagine the wide range of emotions an employee at Community Bridges might go through in the average day. Yet it's important to note that surveys often don't capture that emotional component. The firm uses Ultimate Software's Perception tools to analyse employee sentiment and emotional state, offering a deeper perspective into qualitative responses around stress and other recurring issues. Nichols said it's the difference between getting a vague 'not satisfied' response on a survey and understanding the actual, underlying issue that needs resolution.

CASE STUDY   Understanding employee sentiment in near-real time

What if your organization could understand the top issues for employees across the organization with just a few minutes of analysis?

Surveys are often carried out quantitatively, because it's easy to analyse the responses and come away with trends. For instance, 70 per cent of the organization might be engaged. Or 25 per cent of the firm's employees might be happy with the CEO. The issue is that quantitative data lacks substance and depth, which is where qualitative data comes in. However, the problem with qualitative, or open text, responses in employee surveys is that they are incredibly difficult to evaluate and codify quickly. At the same time, these qualitative data points help provide an additional layer of important information that employers can use to peel back the hierarchical layers and peer into the organization with surprising clarity. A great example of this comes from a healthcare client of an industry-leading HCM technology provider. The firm was facing a series of common challenges, some of them unique to healthcare and others more generally focused on the business.

The 10,000-person firm hired a new CEO and wanted him to hit the ground running. Task number one on his agenda was addressing the entire employee population in a virtual town hall meeting just a few days after starting on the job. The issue was the CEO wanted to speak directly to the challenges and hot buttons for the employees, showing that he was in tune with their needs and that he was dedicated to meeting those needs to the best of his ability. Instead of making assumptions about what was top of mind for the employees, the firm used its technology solution to create a simple survey for employees to complete.

Within a few days of opening the survey, more than 10,000 pieces of feedback flowed in through the system. Historically, at this point the data would either be turned over to a third-party consultant or analysed in-house for trends and other insights. However, instead of having to manually analyse the data for trends, hot spots and other friction points, the system automatically surfaced the most important items by leveraging the system's (named 'Xander' in honour of Alexander Graham Bell) sentiment analysis and natural language processing capabilities.

All survey responses were factored into the equation, highlighting key engagement drivers that mattered most to the employee population in near real time. The very next day, the leadership team was able to speak openly to specific employee concerns and avoid further issues with employee morale by addressing the friction points uncovered by the analysis.

The lesson from this story is pretty powerful. We're now able to gather and act upon in-depth data more rapidly than ever before.

I pointed out earlier in the book that one of the unforeseen benefits of AI tools was helping with the adoption of systems and technologies. By having bots as an interface mechanism, some companies are seeing better usage of their tools. However, what if we looked at bots and AI as a way to help drive research-based best practices in engagement, performance and talent management as a whole? By leveraging the research that exists around the entire employee lifecycle, AI systems could offer managers, arguably the most important touchpoint in the employee experience, insights and advice on how to best drive engagement for their employees.

Performance management and enablement

What makes your performance management process different from those of your competition in the marketplace? Do those practices you use actually help enable better performance, or are they processes that everyone does purely by rote? Research shows that there are some distinct things that high-performing employers do that other firms do not, as Figure 7.1 demonstrates.

Each of these practices creates an opportunity to differentiate how you approach performance management, and the right blend for

Figure 7.1   Performance practices of high-performing companies

Talent practice	Gap analysis: high performers are...
Focus on eliminating weaknesses	25% **less** likely to focus on eliminating weaknesses
Forced/stacked ranking	31% **less** likely to use stacked ranking
Annual goal setting	4% **less** likely to use Prioritize annual goals
More frequent goal setting (two or more sessions annually)	44% **more** likely to do more frequent goal setting
Recognition for performance	37% **more** likely to use recognition to drive performance
In-the-moment manager feedback	29% **more** likely to use in-the-moment feedback
Peer feedback	26% **more** likely to use a peer feedback mechanism
Coaching for development	20% **more** likely to use coaching for development purposes
Focus on strengths	14% **more** likely to focus on employee strengths

SOURCE 2017 Lighthouse Research & Advisory Performance Management, Engagement and Business Results Survey (n = 259)

your company can improve the employee experience and support your corporate culture in a powerful way.

On a more individual level, what separates your best performers from their peers? Can you be specific? In most companies, leaders may have some sense of what makes a great performer, but it's not often spelled out clearly, leaving room for bias. However, even with clear performance metrics, the playing field isn't always level for all parties. For example, a study by Stanford researchers found that women received less developmental or helpful feedback in performance reviews than men (Correll and Simard, 2016).[7] In the research, women were more likely to receive vague praise while men were more likely to receive helpful feedback on how to improve their performance. Additionally, women received more criticism around communication styles than any other job component, and comments about being 'too aggressive' in communication were made to females three times as often as to males. What's intriguing is that male managers didn't look very positive in the findings from this study, but when female managers were examined, they doled out their feedback more evenly to both men and women. Whether that's because they had been on the receiving end of that unhelpful feedback in the past or simply because they are less likely to be biased in their approach, it's interesting to see that this phenomenon is not universal for all leaders.

These kinds of findings clearly indicate an opportunity to incorporate artificial intelligence into the equation. What if an AI-based tool could warn managers when they are giving consistently lower reviews to women than to men? Or to older workers? Or to diverse workers? When I worked as the head of human resources for a technology startup, one of my managers at a remote site was very clear in his dislike for one of our employees who was also in the military part-time. Because of the legal protections provided by the law, he could not punish this person when they required time away from work to perform military duties. At the same time, he looked for every chance he could get to try and 'get even' for what he saw as a thorn in his side. I had to manually examine things like performance reviews to make sure he wasn't making overt or veiled comments about this employee's time away from work, because we were not legally able to utilize that information in our reviews of the person's performance. While it might not be something you've dealt with personally, this isn't an isolated incident and it didn't only happen at my firm.

Consider a secondary process that connects to performance for many firms: compensation reviews. Every year in my role as the HR leader I scheduled a compensation review board meeting between myself and the founders of the company. Once performance review and salary increase data came back from across the organization, we blocked off time to look at the data from a compliance and bias standpoint. Were men consistently given raises in the top 50 per cent, or was it evenly dispersed? What about other diverse employee classes? This exercise was, to be frank, tedious. Yet it had to be done. When there were discrepancies or issues, such as when the top 40 per cent of raises were given to men while women were scattered through the bottom 60 per cent, we had to take steps to correct the issues and balance the scales appropriately. While I'm proud of the fact that we had no complaints or challenges of pay discrimination in my tenure there, I would have been just as happy turning this process over to an algorithm. An AI-based system might have caught things I didn't, such as a manager consistently underrating females on a yearly basis, a subtle departmental issue that affected a minority group of workers. With proper calibration, a system like that might have even been able to recommend adjustments to ensure pay parity among the employees instead of relying on a group of three individuals to manually modify the manager's suggestions.

Much of what has been covered around performance so far has been about preventing biases, yet there's so much more that can be done to actually enable better performance for workers. One of our firm's research studies found that 74 per cent of high-performing firms have a performance management practice that improves engagement levels while low performers are 58 per cent more likely to have an ineffective approach that may actually *hamper employee performance* (Lighthouse Research, 2017).[8] How astounding is it that some firms have created performance management processes that prevent employees from being able to perform at their best? It's funny-yet-not-funny to think about the process we as HR leaders have developed for performance management. When I speak about performance management the audience almost always laughs at the general idea that employees and managers universally hate the process, yet the truth is not far from that statement. In most firms the process of performance management has nothing to do with the intended result. Ask any HR leader and they will tell you that performance management at their firm is designed to help track worker performance and help them improve their results, yet virtually every system I've run across fails to do the second half of that. For sure, we're great at tracking performance in the past. We can talk about someone's past performance all day long. But when it comes to actually enabling them and helping them to be better performers, we stumble. AI technologies can help us to improve this particular aspect of the process, supporting managers at key moments.

For example, one of the challenges mentioned previously is the manager's daily struggle with offering in-the-moment feedback to employees. AI tools can help to keep this practice on a manager's radar so they don't miss opportunities to offer feedback and coaching to employees. While not marketed as a performance management system, the Achievers Listen product includes Allie, a bot that reminds managers that they need to offer feedback to their teams. In addition to reminders, Allie can ask questions, gather and analyse feedback data, suggest action steps and more. Because it's built right into the flow of work by being integrated with systems like Slack and Microsoft Teams, managers don't have to go to a separate system to offer feedback to employees. When I think about one of the biggest challenges of getting managers to adopt a system or process for performance management, the hurdle in many cases comes down to getting them to use another tool that isn't in their daily workflow. From a performance management and feedback perspective, the more we can integrate this process into the ways and channels the manager already uses on a daily basis, the more likely it will be adopted and utilized. Additionally, as we've already said within the book in various places, chatbot notifications can be great nudges for managers to do the things they already know they need to do. I've yet to meet a manager that says, 'I really don't want to give feedback to my employees.' Yet they often don't. If we can help them and keep this top of mind, they're more likely to participate and everyone benefits from those kinds of behaviours.

One of the final components of performance discussions that ties in nicely with the next section is around career development. Workers want to grow and develop, and if they can't envision a future path at your company they will surely envision it somewhere else. Managers need to have conversations with workers about what kinds of development they need, what tasks they enjoy and what career aspirations they might have, but those kinds of things are often lost in the shuffle of tasks and priorities that change from day to day. Managers need to be open to this kind of conversation, but employees really need to drive it. AI technologies can help to bring these discussions to the forefront in a variety of ways as we'll explore below.

The gig economy and team development

In 2013, World Bank Group was in trouble. The firm's leader, Jim Kim, had just put plans in place publicly to cut more than US $400 million in the following decade, leading to a variety of restructuring. One of the key components of this cost cutting? A hiring freeze. The challenge of a hiring freeze is that while new workers can't be brought in, work still has to get done. An innovative solution to this problem was the launch of SkillFinder in 2014 (GovLab, nd).[9] Prior to the launch, there was no way for leaders to drill down into the skills of the 27,000 workers across the firm, forcing them to rely on things like job titles to guess what skills an employee might possess. However, the limitations of that approach are fairly evident: a project manager for a software development team may have wildly different skill sets than a project manager for a nutrition-focused project in one of the company's nonprofit endeavours.

The launch of SkillFinder was focused on helping to create better teams and visibility into employee capabilities across the enterprise. I liken it to an 'eBay for talent', where workers can offer up skills and individuals from across the organization can put up projects that require diverse skills to complete. This was the initial goal and purpose, but leaders quickly realized the system was being used in a way that they hadn't foreseen. In the first year of use, a flurry of activity focused not just on building teams, but on exploring and discovering the skills of peers. According to the firm, 'Managers and employees want to understand better the skills and skills gaps of those who sit across from them in order to inform their work plans.' This internal 'expert network' had been coopted by the employees in order to help grow their understanding of the skills and capabilities of existing team members.

While this programme was launched without the aid of machine learning, it's a great example of a type of process that AI could accomplish better than a human, because in spite of the successes there are still humans doing the matching and selection. One firm that has created technology to solve this problem for a range of employers is Nexus AI The technology helps to surface the best employees for a specific team based on the purpose of the team and the skills of the employees themselves, and it can even tap into external resources like freelancers and contingent workers if needed to supplement the capabilities of the internal workforce (Chowdhry, 2017).[10] According to one interview with the founder of the firm, Nexus AI looks beyond the basic details most project management systems would consider, like someone's skills or their available time and schedule. It also examines dynamics around team interactions and organizational behaviour attributes. For instance, is the leader of the team creating the right environment of psychological safety? Consider also the value of simply having the insights generated by a matching system like this. Employers can understand the volume of requests for a particular skill in a holistic way, potentially seeing trends that could be addressed with training or additional hiring activities.

Systems such as these are unaffected by favouritism and other human biases, which means the matching can happen more quickly and potentially improve things like team diversity and performance. The case study at the end of this chapter demonstrates how Shell uses a similar system, Catalant, to solve its challenges with rapidly developing new teams, making use of the deep, yet dormant skills that many of its workers possess.

Internal talent mobility and career pathing

When I think about internal mobility, the first company that comes to mind is a financial services firm. In an interview with the company, I realized that the firm was in trouble; its struggles also represent the similar issues experienced by a significant portion of the marketplace today. The firm was in an uphill battle with its talent management and talent mobility efforts. In the discussion with the digital services leader for the financial services firm, I learned that of the company's nearly 50,000 employees, the company only had clarity into the actual skills and competencies of about 10 per cent of those people. That left approximately 45,000 workers who were nothing more than a job title on an organizational chart because the firm didn't have granular information about the skills and capabilities of each of those individuals. This lack of clarity was a challenge, because this particular leader had been tasked with developing specialized teams using the existing workforce. This went beyond not knowing how to tap into those employees for team development – it also presented issues with recruiting and learning as well. If you don't know the skills your people have, how can you target gaps with training? Additionally, if you have open roles, how can you promote them to the right people if you're not aware of the capabilities of your existing workers?

The truth is that employees who find another opportunity within your company are more likely to stay, yet employers are notorious for a lack of transparency around job openings internally. Data from one research study shows that more than half of employees say their company makes career opportunities known somewhere between never and occasionally, but only a minority say it's done on a regular basis (Mercer, 2015). This is an issue, because in our extensive analysis at Lighthouse Research of internal talent mobility, we've uncovered a wide variety of use cases, examples and stories that help to illustrate the value of internal mobility.

Chipotle, a fast-casual restaurant chain, reduced store manager attrition by more than 50 per cent when it switched its practice from hiring managers externally to only hiring managers from within the

internal job board

ranks of the existing employee population (NCFSHRM, 2011).[12] Credit Suisse has a programme called Internals First, where recruiters at the company call their own employees about job opportunities before looking to external candidates, which has led to the company saving more than $75 million in hiring and training costs (Harvard Business Review, 2016).[13] When we add to this data from Wharton about how employees who are hired from outside the company cost approximately 20 per cent more money but perform worse on average for their first two years on the job, it becomes clear that hiring from within the ranks of the company is a powerful way to drive better performance and results (Bidwell, 2011).[14]

Several technology vendors sell systems that help to solve this problem. For example, one firm's system guides workers through the process as they look for career opportunities within the firm, helping them get up to speed on what the new job requires. It all starts when employees put in information about their interests, skills and aspirations. Then the system identifies opportunities that match the unique skills fingerprint for each employee. As workers look at opportunities, the system can highlight the gaps between current and future skills in the new career track along with actual learning resources to fill those gaps. The learning component can be actual formal learning content or informal and social learning relationships with mentors and subject matter experts. Think about it from the mentoring and social learning aspect: being able to see the gap between your current and your needed skill set is one thing, but being able to have conversations with subject matter experts and top performers in that job is an exciting prospect. Some technologies even allow workers to work on smaller projects in an effort to stretch and grow their less-developed skill sets. All of these interactions are powered by AI and are scalable, which means that the system can be helping individuals across the firm create their own unique growth and development plans. While at the end of the day managers are going to be involved to support the transition, onboarding and performance components, the finer details of these interactions can be easily managed by a smart algorithm.

Leadership succession is one component of internal mobility that is clearly affected by the advent of AI technologies. If we translate the common issue with bias in hiring selection to succession selection, it's pretty obvious that employers will not make strides at increasing diversity in key leadership roles without major interventions. However, if those decisions are initiated or supported by unbiased algorithms, employers can find better, more diverse candidates for succession than the common method of 'gut feel' that they default to. Additionally, because AI systems can use a wide variety of inputs, they might be able to see patterns that humans can't. For example, a manager might think a candidate is qualified for a leadership role when in reality the system can see that the individual's performance suffered in the past when transitioned to leadership positions, signifying that the person may be better suited to an individual contributor role. Instead of forcing someone into a role that might not fit, the AI can help to guide decisions using a fuller and more accurate picture of their overall performance history.

And just in case you thought we'd get past this topic without bringing up chatbots, there are employers that use bots to help guide employees through these types of conversations about career aspirations. Just like we discussed in Chapter 5 about how bots can help with candidate questions in the talent acquisition process, bots can also assist internal workers looking for that next opportunity. However, the interactions can include even more data and insight into existing employees and career paths since the system user is already an employee. IBM uses its own tools in-house to help employees understand what career opportunities exist, the degree to which their skills match the openings and what other individuals currently hold those types of positions (Hardy-Valee, 2018).[15] The idea that I could, in a company of nearly 400,000 workers, find other individuals across the enterprise who hold jobs I might be interested in is intriguing. The team at IBM believes that managers simply aren't equipped to have transparent conversations about career opportunities. Even if the manager wasn't worried about losing and having to replace a critical employee, which is a common issue, there is a clear trend in individuals wanting to take ownership over their own careers. Even if this means moving beyond the typical career path or career ladder to more of a career 'lattice' structure, workers want some measure of control.

CASE STUDY Algorithms determine teams at Royal Dutch Shell

One of the most common struggles for employers is understanding the breadth, depth and variety of skills across the employee population. Understanding your own team is one thing as a manager, but trying to guess at the skills of hundreds or thousands of employees across the enterprise is another issue entirely. Some companies rely on job titles as a map into what capabilities employees have, using titles as a proxy for skills. So if someone's job title is 'project manager', then we could assume the person is proficient in the use of project management software, budgeting, scheduling and so on. But what if the person's prior job was working as a marketing executive or an operations leader? Those kinds of details don't show up in a job description and without a smarter, more granular method for mapping worker competencies those kinds of insights would go unnoticed.

In the past, when firms wanted to set up a new team to pursue a project, they had to search the employee population based purely on first- or second-hand information to try to identify the right mix of skills and capabilities. The bigger the organization, the more difficult it would be to find the right people. For Royal Dutch Shell, a global oil and gas company with more than 90,000 employees, that would present quite the challenge. So the firm turned instead to an algorithm to help establish the right teams (Schechner, 2017).[16] Shell uses Catalant, a system that helps employers to develop internal talent marketplaces where workers can define their skills using in-depth profiles. Conversely, project leaders can lay out initiatives they need help with so workers have the opportunity to share their expertise in areas that interest them. Shell's adoption of the system started in 2017 and it rolled out the Shell Opportunity Hub within the firm's B2B marketing division with nearly 8,000 employees.

Even as recently as a few years ago, employers would have to reach into the open market and hire an external candidate if it was unable to identify the right internal talent to pull into strategic projects. While there's nothing wrong with hiring to staff a team, this often meant qualified, available and interested internal candidates were passed over simply because of a lack of clarity around capabilities or aspirations. Shell knows it has a deep bench of employees that are willing and able to carry out the projects it has on tap – if only it can find them. Caroline Missen, Business Advisor at Shell, said, 'We're looking at how we can efficiently access and use the diverse talent we already have in Shell' (Schechner, 2017).

Systems like Catalant help employers to manage the process of creating new teams, but they can go further as well. For example, these types of software can help with scheduling and guiding strategic projects through milestones, a process previously reserved for human project managers. One use case for the system at Shell was when the firm needed help looking at digital business models in the car maintenance division of the business. With a few clicks the system scanned available talent within Shell and assigned them to the team.

Another issue with project-based work? A lack of clarity around performance. If workers are not participating in a team with their manager, it is often difficult to get data on how the individuals performed as a part of the initiative or project. The tools Shell uses help to capture that information and ensure a level of transparency around performance that helps with future team development. For instance, if Mary lists a specific skill or expertise in her employee profile but fails to perform on a project, the algorithm can refine the search results to move other candidates higher up the list in future matching attempts.

As we've already seen, there's a fine balance to the influence and authority for people and algorithms in a work situation. The task of project management is heavily process-oriented and therefore a good opportunity to leverage the strengths of an algorithm to select teams and assign tasks without bias in addition to gathering performance data. At the same time, the algorithm is looking for the strongest and best-fit capabilities of the individual employees to predict and create the best-performing team possible. This is a great example of how to blend the best of humans and technology to create better outcomes for the people and the business.

Because talent management touches on so many facets of the employment relationship, the integration of AI into the mix creates ample opportunities to serve up personalized information, recommendations and more. Having an employee's performance data on hand is one thing, but being able to also see where they best contribute to teams, how engaged they are relative to their peers and what succession opportunities exist creates a more complex and complete picture for employers. And as I've said previously, AI is about helping us to make better predictions and decisions. One misstep in the talent management function might be all it takes to lose that star performer to the competition.

In the last few chapters we have covered some of the most important tasks that HR leaders are responsible for: core HR, recruiting, learning and now talent management. But we're not quite through. The next chapter takes a step back from the day-to-day activities and shines a strategic spotlight on areas where you can expect to see challenges in the adoption and usage of AI technologies. While I am an optimist and believe we're better off with these tools at our disposal, that doesn't mean this monumental transition won't come with its own set of challenges. Consider this an opportunity to preempt the inevitable issues by educating yourself thoroughly on critical areas like algorithm aversion, data privacy and more.

Key points

- Employers are understandably excited about the capabilities offered by algorithms, but we must be careful not to automate too much as removing humanity from some processes can lead to backlash in the employee population.

- Managers play a key role in the engagement of employees. Having AI technology on hand to support that relationship, not replace it, is where the true value lies.

- Business leaders can use AI to create a more holistic view of employees and their capabilities, leveraging that information to rapidly build teams, create talent pipelines for key roles and solve business-critical problems with the right mix of skills.

Notes

1 https://www.pbs.org/newshour/economy/uber-drivers-game-app-force-surge-pricing

2 https://www.hrexchangenetwork.com/hr-talent-management/articles/your-biggest-employee-engagement-challenge-is-aft

3 https://www.npr.org/sections/alltechconsidered/2017/06/09/531642304/the-faceless-boss-a-look-into-the-uber-driver-workplace

4 http://news.gallup.com/businessjournal/182792/managers-account-variance-employee-engagement.aspx

5 https://www.octanner.com/content/dam/oc-tanner/documents/white-papers/InfluencingGreatnessWhitepaper.pdf

6 https://www.ultimatesoftware.com/PR/Press-Release/Growing-Non-Profit-Healthcare-Provider-Uses-UltiPro-Perception-to-Build-Trust-Support-Employee-Success

7 https://hbr.org/2016/04/research-vague-feedback-is-holding-women-back

8 https://upstarthr.com/wp-content/uploads/2017/11/LH-High-Value-Performance-Management-Practices-Graphic.jpg

9 http://www.thegovlab.org/static/files/smarterstate/skillfinder.pdf

10 https://www.forbes.com/sites/amitchowdhry/2017/11/13/nexus-ai/#65c561b94012

11 https://www.mercer.com/newsroom/one-in-three-employees-claim-to-have-a-job-rather-than-a-career-new-mercer-survey-finds.html

12 https://ncfshrm.shrm.org/blog/2011/10/internal-promotion-how-chipolte-reduced-turnover-64

13 https://hbr.org/2016/09/why-people-quit-their-jobs

14 http://journals.sagepub.com/doi/abs/10.1177/0001839211433562

15 https://www.ibm.com/blogs/watson-talent/2018/05/hidden-in-plain-sight/

16 https://www.wsj.com/articles/meet-your-new-boss-an-algorithm-1512910800

Challenges of adopting AI technology 08

One million dollars was up for grabs in the competition. The only catch? A team would have to build a chatbot capable of having an extended conversation with a human subject for 20 minutes. That's it. It seems like a fairly simple exercise, right? Any of us could sit down and have a conversation with another person for 20 minutes, but computers have issues with these interactions because of the inherent challenges of processing natural language conversations in real time, having a database of information to refer to and understanding the nuances of human speech. This is why Amazon has laid out an impressive million-dollar Alexa Prize for the team that can create a chatbot capable of having a 20-minute conversation with a human (Vlahos, 2018).[1] In November 2017, the finals for the 2017 competition were happening, including a showdown between the three remaining competitors' chatbots. Judges in a hidden booth were listening intently to live conversations between volunteers and bots, and when the conversation became hung up or no longer made sense, they would push a button to cut off the demonstration. The goal was simple: the longer the bot lasted, the higher it scored in the competition. If any bot lasted to the 20-minute mark, it would win the Alexa Prize.

Within the competition, each team relied on a blend of handcrafted responses and rules-based interactions along with a degree of machine learning to try to generate responses on the fly. Think about each approach like opposite ends of a scale where the ideal balance produces a conversation similar to human speech. On one end is machine learning which analyses conversational context and inputs to make statistically accurate guesses at how to respond to questions. For example, one of the bots in the competition found out that the participant enjoyed a particular movie, so it suggested another movie with the same lead actor and followed it up with a joke about the actor. That data wasn't programmed but instead was pulled from internet conversations and repackaged by the chatbot into the context of the discussion. The other end of the scale is made up of hand-crafted programming rules. These rules and templates help the system to identify acceptable responses to questions and give it time to formulate a coherent response. For instance, one team programmed feedback language into its bot to acknowledge the participant's interests. If the person said, 'Tell me what happened yesterday in Yugoslavia', the system would respond, 'It looks like you want to talk about the news', as the acknowledgement before it moved into responding to the actual request.

In the finals of the competition, each discussion started out as any idle conversation would. The person initiating the conversation would start with, 'Alexa, let's chat.' The game was on from there. The performance of each bot ranged wildly. One of them was tripped up just three minutes into the discussion by the user changing topics in mid-conversation. The second system was able to talk with one participant for seven minutes, but the conversation fell apart when the bot confused the term 'war' with the radio station 'WOR' out of New York during a discussion about global politics and news. The winning chatbot delivered pretty much everything we want a friendly conversation to include: interesting tidbits of information, appropriate jokes and a fun way to pass the time. While it didn't quite reach the 20-minute mark because of a segue into healthcare factoids, the system designed by the University of Washington outperformed the other participants with an average conversation duration of more than 10 minutes, winning the competition even though it fell short of the full Alexa Prize threshold.

This makes for an interesting story, but what's the impact from an HR standpoint? Throughout this book we've talked about bots and their capabilities to support and guide a variety of interactions throughout the candidate and employee experience. However, these bots are mostly driven by the rules-based elements and are not always able to sort out conversational nuances of speech. This example shows some of the most cutting-edge technologies available today in conversational speech, and even with financial incentives and world-class research and developer talent, the tools are not yet capable of having extended conversations. Even with all of the advances in technological capabilities I've observed over the course of researching this book, there is an incredible amount of white space for growth in this area. This is a challenge, of course, but there are other challenges that we must face as we attempt to bring more AI into the workplace. Those challenges include everything from biased systems and a general mistrust of data collection and algorithms to more theoretical questions like when humans should step back into decision making and how we will know to retake control when algorithms begin making more important decisions in the workplace.

Biased systems

In the 2017 Artificial Intelligence Index report, one of the points of analysis was around sentiment of media coverage around AI by year.[2] In 2016, negative coverage of AI spiked to the highest point to date. If we set aside all of the 'AI and robots are coming for our jobs' hyperbole, one of the most common concerns with artificial intelligence is perpetuating bias using algorithms. For example, the 'fake news' that crops up on social media is delivered to us based on our own preferences and habits. If I already believe the sky is purple or that a particular politician is untrustworthy, and I read about or share those topics on social media, the platform I'm using will offer up even more examples and sources of information confirming those types of biases, further shutting me off from a balanced view of the world. The bias I already have is being reinforced and further deepened by algorithms giving me what I want. This personal example may seem relatively innocuous, but there's a darker side that impacts the workplace as well.

One day a Harvard professor was working on a project and Googled her own name to find something. However, she was shocked by what appeared in the sponsored advertisement section of the page. In the little box she read 'Latanya Sweeney Arrest Record'. Knowing that she'd never had an arrest record, she clicked through to see what it led to. Ultimately it was just another pay-per-click advertisement on Google's search results, but it piqued her curiosity (Sweeney, 2013).[3] In the following months, Sweeney conducted a research study to understand how and why the ads appeared, and realized through her experiments that 'black-sounding' names were much more likely to return an 'arrest record' result in a search while 'white-sounding' names were more likely to return more benign results. Remember, computers only use what they are programmed with, and if more people are clicking on the alleged arrest records then the algorithm will prioritize those in search results pages. These types of algorithms reinforce what we already believe, whether it's correct or not.

Another side of this is making predictions based on biased algorithms. For example, in the chapter on talent acquisition I talked about using AI as an unbiased tool for matching people to job openings. We should expect this to be fair, right? It doesn't take into account gender, race, or age when matching a candidate's resume or skills with a job advertisement. Yet it's possible that those predictions and suggestions the algorithm is making are entirely biased, depending on the models used to train the system. Consider this example: you work for an investment bank that draws a significant portion of its workforce from prestigious MBA programmes at Ivy League universities. You use an algorithm that is designed to find candidates who match the high-performing workers you already have. If those workers all have similar backgrounds like Ivy League schools, specific zip codes, or other components, you may be discriminating against minorities and women in your selection process. Think about it for a second. The system's goal is to screen a batch of candidates and look for individuals similar to those that already have jobs at your firm. If you have an overwhelming population of young, white males in your firm, the system will try to select that same population.

It's a bit unsettling, but it also can serve as a reminder to have regular check-ups on our existing processes and practices (whether AI-powered or not). It's also a reminder that humans can never fully let go of the reins (more on this in the section below). If our current approach is biased to some degree, then we need to take steps to change it, and the first step is to identify whether the approach is biased or not. Early in 2018, Pymetrics, an assessment company focusing on the talent acquisition market, open-sourced its AI tool for detecting algorithm bias (Johnson, 2018).[4] Companies can use this tool to identify if an algorithm is selecting based on biased factors or not. While we would hope that vendors in the space would be accounting for these kinds of things, that isn't always the case. Tools like the one Pymetrics released will help to solve these issues with biased algorithms, however common they may be.

An important point to remember is that AI does not inherently understand the concept of bias. The algorithm runs an operation, comes to a conclusion and presents that information. It's up to us as developers and implementers of AI solutions to be aware of bias and where it might rear its ugly head. Biased algorithms are a real danger and one that we must be vigilant about as more AI technologies enter the workplace. After all, the worst that can happen to the system is to be shut down. However, the human in charge of making the decisions based on the system's recommendations can lose their job if the errors and decisions are grossly biased and unaddressed by the ultimate decision maker, resulting in unfair and discriminatory employment practices.

Technological complacency

If I threw out a random 10-digit number for you to remember, how well do you think you would do? This used to happen regularly when we would gather a phone number from a friend or relative, but today we just plug that into our phones and move on. I've actually run across friends that forgot the phone numbers of their own spouses when they lost access to their mobile device! In the next chapter I point out how things like creativity must be nurtured and developed if we want to maintain a human edge with our soft skills, but a more basic question is whether AI handicaps our ability to think. If so, what can we do about it, if anything? Kurt Marko, a writer for

Diginomica, writes about this in the context of human skills and how they atrophy over time. Marko (2018) asserts that our continued reliance on automation will lead to increasing losses in the skills we needed to accomplish those tasks prior to automation. Instead of just relying on the systems until human intervention is needed, they should be designed in such a way that continuously reinforces our skill development and refinement. Additionally, he points out that 'convenience is the death of innovation' if we try to automate away opportunities for human creativity and epiphany.[5]

In a conversation with Dale Kennedy, an HCM product expert at Infor, we discussed this concept in terms of self-driving vehicles. Kennedy believes that AI has the capability to improve human resources dramatically not just through automating tedious processes but by providing key information and insights that talent leaders need at critical times. However, he explained that as vehicles get smarter and smarter at driving autonomously, there is less and less need for human interaction at the wheel. This can create critical weaknesses in our ability to navigate situations and take over in times when the vehicle runs into an unpredictable situation. Our senses and skills can become dull without practice. Consider the example of the SourceCon Grandmaster Challenge winner Randy Bailey profiled in Chapter 5. He was able to beat the recruiting algorithm with a mix of tenacity and ingenuity because his searching and critical thinking skills are sharp and finely honed. If he was only using algorithms to automate sourcing, searching and communicating with candidates, then he would not have been able to beat the machine in my opinion.

In another example related to our topic, let's imagine that your firm begins using an algorithm to suggest pay rates for new offers based on historical compensation data, market trends, company performance, employee turnover data and other relevant inputs. The system was implemented in the hope of levelling the playing field and eliminating the pay gap between male and female workers. The technology seems to be working perfectly, but after a few years the system begins suggesting higher and higher pay rates in job offers because it sees that employee turnover drops as wages increase, even though the business is not improving enough to cover the costs. If you were running HR at this firm, how would you know when to take back control? And, if you took control, would you know how to solve this problem after several years of letting that skill lapse? In this scenario recruiters and/or hiring managers would have to be retrained on how to negotiate salary with candidates, but the HR team would also have to revitalize its knowledge and capabilities around compensation best practices, trends in pay transparency and other related factors. A metaphor that makes this challenge easier to grasp is to imagine your firm has a single person in charge of running all decisions around learning technology and content strategy. Then that person leaves the firm without notice. How would you recover?

It really comes down to the fact that AI has the option to make us less intelligent, if we let it. In a conversation with the Head of Talent for a public utility, she explained that her firm's leadership team had purchased a machine learning tool to help provide insight into a particular business challenge. However, it quickly became apparent that the business leaders weren't using the system to help support their decisions – they were using its recommendations *as* the decision. There was no oversight, no input or no pushback on the recommendations of the system, despite the fact that no algorithm is 100 per cent accurate all the time. She was frustrated at their inability to see that the system was meant to be a decision support tool – a predictive tool – not a decision-making tool. Her fear was that the team would become too reliant on the system, fail to realize when it was leading them astray and be too far removed from the problem to make any meaningful change to rectify the issue.

The core question I want you to consider is not just if we'll realize when we need to put our hands back 'on the wheel' in these situations. The bigger question is what we might be losing in the process. The answer is to ensure that even in a process we're automating, we still have human oversight. We avoid black box algorithms that compute and make predictions with no context or clarity around how the decisions were made. We prioritize human skills like creativity, collaboration and critical thinking so that we don't lose that edge that allows us to overcome a wide variety of challenges in the workplace, regardless of what they might be.

Algorithm aversion

Did you know that Gallup's data says that more than nine out of ten people who take a new job do so outside their own company (Rigoni and Nelson, 2015)?[6] This has always puzzled me, especially in larger companies, because there is a plentiful supply of capable talent for employers to take advantage of, yet they look outside for hiring decisions. When this is combined with the data from the Wharton study we looked at earlier in the book that shows external hires cost more and perform worse, it shines a glaring light on one of the most common decisions we make. As organizations and leaders, we're more likely to look for an external candidate, in part, because we don't know all their flaws. We've never seen them fail. We believe, for some reason, that a hire from outside the company is going to perform better. This is a close parallel to the concept of algorithm aversion we're going to discuss below.

Algorithm aversion has a confounding effect on our hope to adopt and leverage AI-powered software in the workplace, and it is similar to the example of prioritizing external hiring. In essence, algorithm aversion is the term to describe our mistrust of the predictions algorithms offer. In several studies, researchers have shown that we are less likely to believe in algorithms than in human judgment, especially if we have seen them err (Dietvorst, Simmons and Massey, 2014).[7] This is the same decision we make when we avoid promoting our internal workers and instead seek an outside candidate for a role. While the experiments were focused on several different prediction scenarios, let's apply this to the world of HR that we live in. As you dig into some of the results and information from the experiments below, look at them through the lens of predicting the right candidate, helping a worker choose the right development path, or finding the right engagement method for an employee. Try to look at these findings through a common prediction challenge you face, because it will make the concepts more tangible.

In one set of experiments, participants had to choose whether to put their belief in an algorithm or in a human for a series of forecasting activities. The researchers found that we as humans are much more likely to believe in our own abilities over those of an algorithm, and those differences became even more pronounced when a participant saw the algorithm make an error in its predictions. While we might give our co-workers or even ourselves a break when we make a poor decision, we're less likely to give an algorithm a break when that happens. The reason this is significant in the context of the workplace is that algorithms will increasingly be used to support decisions and even make decisions in some instances, and if there is a fundamental distrust of the information the algorithms suggest, then adoption and usage will not go as planned. Additionally, let's say an algorithm is being used to help with removing bias from hiring decisions. If that algorithm is avoided because the hiring manager doesn't think it's making good suggestions, then the biased hiring processes of old will continue to proliferate.

To get a more nuanced view of the specific issues that humans have with their algorithmic counterparts, participants in the studies were asked to rate the performance of humans against that of algorithms on a specific group of attributes. The responses offer an incredibly nuanced perspective of how we perceive ourselves relative to software models. For example, participants said that algorithms were better at avoiding obvious mistakes and weighting information in a consistent manner. However, those in the experiments rated themselves as superior in detecting exceptions, finding the 'hidden gems' the software overlooks and learning from mistakes. Across the four experiments the results of these measurements were sometimes less pronounced, but one specific characteristic came out in favour of human judgement every time: getting better with practice. So, what does this have to say about us as humans? We give computers credit for things that are obvious: they are unbiased and more likely to be consistent, and that consistency can mean they don't make those silly or obvious mistakes that humans might by accident or in a tired state. On the other hand, we wildly overvalue characteristics in ourselves. We think we can detect exceptions in data, even though computers are much better at detecting exceptions in large volumes of data. We think we learn from past mistakes, but how many times have you made a mistake more than once before you realized the root cause of the mistake? And finally, we believe we get better with practice. While that may be the case, we also need to acknowledge the fact that computers can get progressively better with practice and they do not share some of our needs for things like rest.

But one of the conclusions of the authors at the end of the study was that it didn't explore deeply enough into what it would take for humans to believe in an algorithm. Yes, we know that people are less likely to believe in an algorithm than in humans, especially after we've seen an algorithm make a mistake. But how could we shift this perception so that users actually trust what algorithms offer? In a later exploration of this concept, one of the authors took on this challenge with interesting results. Dietvorst built upon the original study by allowing participants in the experiments to use algorithmic models to make predictions, but then those participants were allowed to modify the algorithms to a slight degree (Dietvorst, Simmons and Massey, 2016).[8] The results are fascinating. When those in the experiment had an opportunity to modify the algorithm, they were more likely to be satisfied with the predictions of the algorithm and, accordingly, more likely to use the algorithm in the future. But the interesting part is the degree to which those modifications could occur. Even if those modifications were insignificant, participants were more likely to believe in the algorithms. To explain, consider the following scenario.

Let's say you were going to predict who is the right succession candidate for an executive role. To begin, your algorithm presents a slate of candidates. As we've already seen, you have an innate distrust of algorithms, but as with the above experiment, you have an opportunity to modify the algorithm to some degree by making sure it takes into account the factors *you* think are important to making the right selection decision. Even if the inclusion of those factors doesn't change the slate of candidates one bit, you're still more likely to believe in the predictions it makes. I liken it to the example of when someone has to speak up in a meeting to 'say their piece'. Even if their statements don't fundamentally alter the direction of the decision being made, the person feels better knowing they had their opportunity to weigh in on the topic.

This idea of using modifiable algorithms that accept user inputs (even if it doesn't change the outcome) is one of the answers to solving this problem of algorithm aversion. Another is to openly examine the performance of the algorithm, comparing and contrasting with the human decisions. The more we can shine a light on this bias, the more likely we can overcome it. We know that algorithms and software can offer better forecasts than humans, yet we have a tendency to discount the value of those predictions in favour of our 'gut' or our 'instinct'. In areas like predicting medical issues, this scepticism could be costly. In terms of hiring or promotion decisions, it could be the difference between success or failure. Or, in some cases, this 'gut feel' approach could lead to less diversity and higher risk of litigation. Overall, it demonstrates a key hurdle between where we are today and where we want to go as an employer population. If we want the benefits of AI technology like rapid processing, unbiased recommendations and so on, then we need to be willing to trust the recommendations and predictions those technologies can offer. Otherwise it will be like running a race with your ankles tied together: you might eventually get to the finish, but it won't be fast and it won't be pretty.

These findings could signify a few things that we need to be aware of. First of all, we don't really trust algorithms very much. Over time, as we see the recommendations are relatively accurate, that trust will grow, just like a relationship with a new co-workers blossoms as we build trust. That said, the idea that we need to be heard reinforces yet again the concept from the Uber drivers' rebellion against their own algorithm. When employers rely too heavily on algorithms to make choices, the people who are accustomed to being listened to are going to feel left out. Imagine you are the expert on a certain topic in your workplace and your employer buys a new system that automates recommendations that you normally provide. Even if this doesn't displace you from your position, it's bound to put some measure of strain on you as your voice becomes less and less 'heard' relative to the algorithm.

Because we as HR leaders have insight into the HR operations at our firms, we have the unique opportunity to see these adoptions as they cut across the employee population. We can look for ways to ensure the people are still a part of the decisions to whatever degree is necessary. Plus, it would be wise to think through what will happen in the inevitable instance where the human worker disagrees with something that an algorithm predicts. Who do you side with? How do you do it in such a way that you don't completely disengage the worker, dismantling the value they've built around their role and recommendations over time? Continued research in this field will help to shed light on how we can work with our AI-based systems and not against them, but it's also up to us to help lay a foundation of trust by adopting and utilizing these types of systems wherever they can add value.

Data privacy and AI

One variable in the equation that may encourage workers to be less trusting in artificially intelligent systems is data privacy. Data from the Sierra-Cedar HR Systems Survey shows a statistically significant correlation between employers with a data risk and information security strategy that includes HR systems and those employers that have an interest in machine learning tools (Sierra-Cedar, 2017).[9] This makes sense as employers with a keen eye for information security realize the treasure trove of data that resides in the HR information systems. The information in those systems requires protection, but has your firm even thought about how it would answer the common questions around this data, how it's collected, whether or not it's shared with other entities and what it's used for?

Several years ago, I was speaking on a panel at a conference. The topic of the session was HR analytics, and the room was packed with business executives from firms around the globe trying to understand how to adopt analytics in a way that fit their unique needs. A woman stood up during the question and answer portion and asked the panel how she could take advantage of analytics when her employees wouldn't allow it. Intrigued, I asked her to elaborate. It turned out that her firm was based in Germany, and the worker council had a firm grip on what data was being collected from employees and who could access it. In this example she had led a project to gather data in an employee engagement survey with the goal of improving the conditions and work environment for the employees, but when the firm tried to bring in its third-party consulting partner to analyse the data, things got tricky. The council would not grant access to the third party to access and analyse the data on the firm's behalf. Because of that decision, the firm would either have to hire a new employee on the HR team just to help work through the survey data or shelve the whole thing, wasting the funds invested in the development and capture of the survey.

At the time, I'll admit this example seemed to be a little 'out there' for me. I remember wondering if employees really cared that much about who saw their data and what it might be used for. Yet times have changed. More and more public data breaches have caused people to be more careful about who has their information and what they can do with it. For example, in 2017 a data breach at Equifax led to the exposure of personal information from 143 million people. (Federal Trade Commission, nd).[10] Additionally, one online source points out that of the nearly 10 trillion records lost or stolen in data breaches since 2013, only 4 per cent of them were encrypted, effectively rendering the data useless to hackers (Breach Level Index, 2018).[11]

If we add new laws like the General Data Privacy Regulation (GDPR) enacted in the EU in 2018, this landscape is definitely changing. GDPR rocked the HR world for months in advance of its adoption as talent acquisition and HR leaders looked for information on how to prepare for the law's implementation and requirements for data protection, and even today the aftershocks are still being felt in terms of demand for training and information about what GDPR really means for global employers and the data they collect and use. For example, employers using recruiting technologies that store information on applicants have much tighter restrictions on the data. Employers need to be very clear around the areas of consent, disclosure and retention of data (Maurer, 2018).[12] Another interesting point in the GDPR law includes a requirement to provide the right to an explanation. That's right – consumers now have a legally protected right to ask for an explanation of the algorithms that impact their lives (Amornvivat, 2018).[13] So, while the original request from the German-based HR executive seemed to be out of place at the time, in hindsight it was a foreshadowing of the concern around employee data privacy that was to come.

Despite it throwing me off a bit, the answer I gave to that leader is still applicable today, and perhaps even more so. While I didn't have a simple answer for getting the council to change its mind, I did encourage the HR executive to be very clear with the employees about what kinds of data the company collected and how it would be used. The example I gave her was around video streaming. Regardless of the video streaming service you use, they all collect data about your viewing patterns, preferences and more. The fact that all of that information is being captured, stored and analysed should worry us to some degree, right? After all, research in the 2016 Global Internet Phenomena Report shows that more than half of downstream internet traffic for North America comes from just two sources: Netflix (35 per cent) and YouTube (17 per cent) (Sandvine).[14] Yet we're not worried. Why? Because if our video streaming service knows us, then it can offer us better content recommendations. We spend less time browsing and more time enjoying. Or, if our favourite e-commerce website knows our buying patterns and preferences, then it can help us keep our cupboards full of the things we like best. There is a clear line of sight between the information gathered and the value we receive back from those systems. The question we should all be asking as HR and business leaders is what kind of value we're offering back to our employees and how we can communicate that so they understand and approve of the way we're using their data. In order to utilize AI to its fullest extent and make accurate predictions about the future, we need to have access to comprehensive data sources. This issue of data privacy is cropping up at just the right time, because it will force employers to be clear about the data they gather, how they plan to use it and (if they're smart) how that will benefit the employees and candidates the data comes from.

System integration is lacking

I read several years ago about a company that flies over retail shopping centres taking real-time photos of parking lots as a way to predict earnings. The fuller the lot, the more the earnings should be, on average. What if we could also integrate this information into scheduling and staffing practices of retail stores so we knew on a more granular level how many people to schedule for a particular shift and when to ping contingent labour sources that could provide resources quickly? The problem with that is a lack of integration. Many of the ideas presented in this book hinge on the idea that systems talk with each other. And I'm not talking about 'upload a spreadsheet file and we'll update the system' kinds of integration. I'm talking about real-time or near real-time access to information from a variety of systems, both inside and outside of HR.

These integrations form a sort of 'connective tissue' that enables better decisions. The more information you have, the better the prediction you can offer, right? And if we're in a profession that lives and dies by the predictions we make, then shouldn't we want our systems to have better connections? In recent years I've seen technology firms take steps to open up their application programming interfaces (APIs) and enable better connectivity for partners and others, yet this is still not a strong capability for most vendors. APIs are a way for technology providers to allow other systems to access portions of the database, enabling data to flow in from one system to the other or even bidirectionally if designed for that purpose. The problem? The artificial intelligence many vendors are offering is making recommendations based only on data that lives in their system, because they don't have the ability to read and access other systems. That said, some vendors are trying to make headway in this area by prioritizing this. The takeaway for you is to talk with your own vendors and potential future partners to let them know this is a priority for you. Imagine being able to see performance, learning, survey feedback and compensation data in one place so that you understand if you're paying your managers in an equitable way. Or having your learning and recruiting systems connected so that your internal employees can see the open jobs and the training they could take to improve their competitiveness for those open roles.

Another example to wrap up with here is chatbots. E W Scripps is a 4,000-employee firm that's been in business since 1878. In a recent presentation by the firm's head of human resources, he explained how the firm had connected its chatbot into a variety of HR systems so that employees could access virtually any information for pay, leave, benefits or policies simply by conversing with the bot. This goes beyond simply answering questions based on a pre-defined list of common issues employees face and allows the system to automate much more of the process (LeapGen, 2018).[15]

This lack of connectivity among business and HR systems is a challenge. It won't be solved overnight but the good news is that unlike some of the other challenges presented here that are based on human behaviours and are difficult to change, this is a technological issue. Like any technology problem, this can be solved. The more mature the connections become, the better the AI will become. The better the AI becomes, the more value it will produce for business leaders.

CASE STUDY   Beware the trolls: a cautionary tale of releasing AI into the wild

On 23 March 2016, Tay entered the world. Tay was a bot designed by Microsoft to mimic a 16-year-old teen girl's personality and interaction style on the web. This was to be accomplished by having Tay mimic the speech patterns of Twitter users around the world interacting with the bot. The concept was interesting – can a bot learn to be more human by interacting with humans? In the end, it turns out that trolls, people who post inflammatory messages online for their own entertainment, were the ones that sank Tay's prospects for the future.

At the end of the experiment, Tay was repeating racist remarks and making up original offensive content as well (West, 2016).[16] One might imagine that this experiment took place over the course of several months, with the software being corrupted over time by the volume of negative interactions. In reality, it took less than 24 hours for the AI-powered bot to devolve from a cheerful teen into a hate-spouting monster. Some people, and certainly the programming team from Microsoft, would claim that this is not a fair example because users attempted to 'hack' the bot by intentionally providing leading questions, false information and improper language in a stream that built up the system's knowledge base and awareness of the world. Because this occurred over such a short time, that volume of (bad) information became the dominant portion of the system's programming.

For practical purposes, AI is essentially like an infant. It requires specialized care and 'feeding', especially in the earliest days after it is released into the world. There is great potential, but there is also great danger, as the AI has no awareness of right and wrong. Microsoft's experiment with Tay is a great example of how employers and other firms should not launch tools into public forums without first considering the implications of bad actors interacting with the system. Whether for humour or other more serious purposes, users fed Tay so much negative information that it never really recovered.

Despite the challenges...

In spite of the challenges outlined here, in previous chapters we've explored the significant value that artificial intelligence technologies can provide. More than ever before, I'm convinced of the paradoxical nature of technology adoption. In order to adopt technology that can help eliminate some of the human error, we need to take a very human approach to change management, influencing others to get that technology in place. It's perhaps even more applicable here in this discussion of AI and algorithms as they are more likely to filter out those human 'issues', like biases, around decision making that other technologies never really touched. Accountants have a general ledger that tells the financial truth. Marketers have their customer relationship management and marketing automation tools that highlight prospect interests and activities. But HR software? We deal with the grey areas of people decisions, which are usually much less clear-cut than some of these other examples.

When we think about bringing artificial intelligence technologies into the workplace, we might not run into issues like Microsoft did with Tay. How many of us really need to be integrating a fake teen AI into the rhythm of our workforce communications? However, we will inevitably run into people who try to stretch the system and find its loopholes. For instance, there are countless examples in forums online where users have attempted to have off-script conversations with chatbots, offering up screenshots of the interactions for the comedic value. We intuitively want to find the edges, the holes and the issues with technology as it helps us to prove that we're more human and 'better', by whatever subjective measure we're using at the time of the estimation.

During one interview with Cecile Leroux, an executive at Ultimate Software, she explained that the company's approach to AI development was less about automation and more about augmentation. In other words, it's really about helping today's HR leaders do great things in better ways instead of just automating manual tasks, which brings to mind images of robots replacing humans. In a profession that is supposed to be the most human-centric function within an organization, it's worth remembering that sentiment as it can change how people perceive the advance of AI and the value it can bring. During the early 1800s, English Luddites revolted in an attempt to protect their jobs and destroy automation machinery in the weaving mills. While that sort of outcry is less likely today, it's no less important to think about the perceptions of the workforce when more and more of the workload is being offloaded to algorithms and computers. Especially when those decisions are critically important, such as those surrounding hiring, training, succession and more.

This goes back to the conversation about the AI Effect in Chapter 2. Humans want to feel like they are different or better in some way than technology, so we make an effort to discount advances in artificial intelligence technology by writing off improvements as something less than intelligence. In other words, we keep moving the bar that defines 'intelligence' every time an algorithm or computer meets the bar. It's that need to differentiate ourselves that pushes some people to dig into a bot's inner workings or feed it information that may change its behaviours. We need to expect some level of this when AI becomes a more integrated part of the workplace. The backlash, for lack of a better term, might not be as severe as we saw in the Uber driver 'rebellion' example. Workers might not be so frustrated and powerless that they seek out ways to fight back and sabotage the algorithms that make your workplace function. However, it's foolish to expect complete acceptance by everyone. Additionally, it's important to remember that in the Age of AI (if I'm allowed to offer such a grandiose moniker), the human component is still an essential piece of the puzzle. As John Roese, the President and Chief Technical Officer of Dell EMC, put it, '[Workers] understand that AI and machine learning will eventually disappear into the infrastructure, becoming second nature. They know that machines are non-human and that human ingenuity is irreplaceable' (Banham, 2018).[17] I have repeatedly stressed and provided example after example within the book that this is not an either/or solution, it's an *and* solution. We need people and technology, and each has a distinct set of strengths that we can take advantage of to solve problems and advance toward our goals as business leaders. As we'll explore in the next chapter, the ability for us as humans to use our skills to remain relevant, competitive and valuable will become increasingly important as the level of automation increases in the workplace.

Key points

- Bias is a real and present danger in decision-making processes, and while bias has always been an issue, we need to be careful not to hand off our decisions to an algorithm without clearly understanding how predictions and recommendations are made and if bias is inherent or not.

- As humans, we want to trust our instincts, even if they've been shown to be incorrect in the past. The concept of algorithm aversion may slow adoption of automated technologies, but adoption will certainly increase as we define clear links between the outcomes and the value these tools can provide.

- Data privacy and security have never been more of an issue than in today's workplace. With more data than ever before being created, stored and accessed, employers are creating liability for themselves. Understanding legal requirements and how they apply is a good first step. Leaders should also prioritize these components for internal technology teams and for software partners.

Notes

1 https://www.wired.com/story/inside-amazon-alexa-prize/

2 https://aiindex.org/2017-report.pdf

3 https://papers.ssrn.com/sol3/papers.cfm?abstract_id=2208240

4 https://venturebeat.com/2018/05/31/pymetrics-open-sources-audit-ai-an-algorithm-bias-detection-tool/

5 https://diginomica.com/2018/02/21/beware-the-ai-risks-of-over-automation-and-hyper-convenience/

6 https://news.gallup.com/businessjournal/186311/making-career-moves-americans-switch-companies.aspx

7 http://opim.wharton.upenn.edu/risk/library/WPAF201410-AlgorthimAversion-Dietvorst-Simmons-Massey.pdf

8 https://papers.ssrn.com/sol3/papers.cfm?abstract_id=2616787

9 https://sierra-cedar.com/wp-content/uploads/sites/12/2018/01/Sierra-Cedar_2017-2018_HRSystemsSurvey_WhitePaper.pdf

10 https://www.ftc.gov/equifax-data-breach

11 https://breachlevelindex.com

12 https://www.shrm.org/resourcesandtools/hr-topics/talent-acquisition/pages/gdpr-eu-data-law-hr-recruiting-shrm.aspx

13 https://www.bangkokpost.com/opinion/opinion/1415298/is-it-possible-to-be-too-data-driven-

14 https://www.sandvine.com/hubfs/downloads/archive/2016-global-internet-phenomena-report-latin-america-and-north-america.pdf

15 https://www.youtube.com/watch?v=1H8X3Ac9fgQ&t=14s

16 https://qz.com/653084/microsofts-disastrous-tay-experiment-shows-the-hidden-dangers-of-ai/

17 https://www.delltechnologies.com/en-us/perspectives/easing-in-the-robots-how-to-confront-employee-fears/?elqTrackId=fbd4f354b02041bc9d6ce68ab8ab0cd4&elq=ccd8ec09942649e998e57f0d73a4ba18&elqaid=12289&elqat=1&elqCampaignId=41310

HR skills of the future

When a pathologist needs to diagnose cancer, it requires painstaking scrutiny of biopsy samples to identify cancerous cells. This is the proverbial search for a needle in a haystack, since there could be millions of healthy cells and just a few cancerous ones in any given sample, if cancer is even present in the sample at all. A series of experiments unveiled by Harvard in 2016 involving the analysis of breast cancer tissue cells showed us a stunning set of results (Wanjek, 2016).[1] Teams were assigned the task of identifying metastatic cancer cells because breast cancer is one of the most common types of cancer in addition to being one of the most deadly. The task itself holds significance beyond simple identification, because these types of cells are typically gathered in a biopsy where cancer is suspected but not yet confirmed. Therefore, getting better results at this stage of the process can improve life expectancy for those who have breast cancer.

Within the context of the experiment, the team's artificial intelligence algorithm spotted cancer with 92 per cent accuracy. However, when compared with human pathologists, the AI fell slightly behind. Human experts were able to spot the cancer cells with 96 per cent accuracy. However, this isn't another 'us versus them' story of humans and machines. The real success story happened when the team partnered up both resources to answer the question: are we better together? The answer was clear – in the partner experiments, blending the algorithm with human judgement led to identification of more than 99 per cent of cancerous biopsies. The repercussions are critical: for that 3 per cent of women who would have been misdiagnosed by human pathologists, this could give them a fighting chance.

What do these types of experiments mean? Beyond the obvious answer that humans and machines complement each other's capabilities, this points to something deeper. This kind of finding highlights the fact that what we need from a doctor may be changing. In this example, it's possible that AI would not be able to identify more rare forms of cancer or would not be able to compute an erroneous image, potentially missing a critical diagnosis. In those cases the images could be flagged for human intervention. While they still need to be able to verify a computer's output, doctors will spend less time doing that type of work and more time doing other tasks, many of which could be patient-facing, which may shift the type of skills necessary for success in the medical field. With all due respect to the lovable healthcare robot Baymax from Disney's Big Hero Six, if I was going to receive a diagnosis of a serious health issue, I'd want to get that from a living, breathing human being, not an unfeeling machine. For some tasks, human intervention is not only a good idea in general, it's demanded by the population being served. This shift is inherently similar to the one facing the HR profession and the business more broadly.

Additionally, the renewed focus on soft skills relative to hard skills is something we can't ignore. Doniel Sutton, Global Head of People for PayPal, believes that out of all the skills that the firm's workforce can have, agility is the most important (Gilchrist, 2018).[2] Across the company, Sutton says that agility is the single most critical skill that helps workers to stand out from the crowd and succeed. From bouncing back against ever-present change to learning on the fly, agility encapsulates much of what makes workers successful today. You might imagine the head of hiring and development decisions for a technology firm would say that some coding language or development methodology was the biggest factor, but instead it's a soft skill. Therefore, in a world of increasing automation, what sort of skills are necessary to drive the future of work? How will the demand for hard or soft skills fluctuate based on the increasing capabilities of bots, algorithms and machines? Will soft skills become the currency of the future?

There are two ways to approach these types of questions. The first is to ask what types of things humans can do that machines can't, at least at this current stage of development. However, there are stories almost daily about how these kinds of barriers are being broken down by new robots and tools being developed across the globe. For example, Boston Dynamics' robot can open doors (Simon, 2018).[3] Additionally, the

Henn na Hotel in Japan is almost entirely staffed by robots (The Guardian, 2015).[4] A better question might be to consider how humans can augment what machines can do. This is interesting in itself because we've long seen the equation from the other perspective: how can machines augment what humans can do? Shifting this perspective can guide us toward the right skills that matter not just today, but also into the future as more and more of what we do is able to be automated.

In reality, there's no true way to know just how much automation will change the workplace. Estimates are just that – educated guesses. Earlier in the book I pointed out the search engine optimization example of how jobs change and new ones are created that we couldn't even foresee. However, let's suspend disbelief for a bit and explore some of the research that exists, looking at the big picture thinking behind just how much automation could potentially impact the workplace. If it helps, consider these numbers in the context of direct impact on your entire HR team, if not the whole organization. For example, if a study says to expect 40 per cent automation, consider what that means in the context of your HR function. Would you expect to see 40 per cent fewer people? Have 40 per cent more impact on the business? What would that translate into in terms of creating a more personalized or high-touch employee experience?

As an example, McKinsey reports that nearly half of all work could be automated by 2055 (Caughill, 2017).[5] With all due respect to McKinsey and others that have provided these estimates, they are nothing more than educated guesses that can't be proven or disproven today. While this specific example shows a negative future, there are others that show a more even split about what might occur.

In an analysis more closely related to HR, one European firm surveyed HR practitioners to understand their own perceptions of what AI might mean for the profession (Goetgebuer, 2017).[6] The report pointed out that employers will be looking for different types of competencies from candidates as time progresses, because different skills will be necessary in a world with greater automation. Those skills include the ability to solve complex, challenging problems, a keen focus on service, critical thinking and people management. Respondents in the survey were almost evenly split on several fronts, including whether AI would lead to increases or decreases in jobs, whether HR's role in the business would grow or diminish, and whether AI was a threat or an opportunity.

Additionally, in a study of nearly 2,000 experts in technology and market trends, the Pew Research Center found that this group was evenly split on whether the advances in artificial intelligence would eliminate jobs or not (Smith and Anderson, 2014).[7] In the study, key leaders at a variety of technology firms pointed out the opportunity for job creation with the new robots, algorithms and learning systems in place, explaining that these new jobs might be drastically different than what has existed in the past. If I can put on my futurist cap for a moment, I believe this job creation can also apply to the HR profession. For instance, in the learning and development profession, one of the newer roles for forward-thinking employers is a learning experience designer. These are specialists designing learning experiences that engage learners with content formats, types and delivery mechanisms that create additional value beyond static, transactional methods. Just as the learning and development profession now has individuals focused on learning experience design, it's possible that enterprise organizations will have key positions focused on designing candidate and employee experiences that create emotional and rational connections with every individual. Building these experiences will require not only advanced versions of the AI technologies we have today but also the human intuition necessary to guide those technologies to successful outcomes.

The takeaway here is that whether the audience is a group of HR professionals doing the work or a group of high-level thinkers and academics with a broader view of the world, both groups are equally puzzled about what the future might hold in this area. What matters on a more fundamental level is the expectation and anticipation of change and what it means for the workplace. Companies will change. Jobs will change. People will be forced to change along with them. In virtually every organization, HR is the one tasked with change management. However, one thing I've learned over the course of my career is that HR can often fail to see the impact that might be happening within its own function. What skills will be unnecessary, or at the very least deprioritized, over the course of time?

Consider the following example of human performance that leaves us awestruck. In 2006, Alex Haraguchi sat in a public location with his eyes closed, talking. And talking. And talking. For more than 16 hours, Haraguchi recited 100,000 digits of pi from memory. For most of us that took mathematics, rounding pi to 3.14 was good enough to get the job done, but this Japanese man has dedicated a significant portion of his life to memorizing digits of pi. However, a computer could easily list pi digits beyond 100,000 without requiring years of training and 16-plus hours of vocalization (Bellos, 2015).[8] One of my new standby jokes when it comes to this discussion of shifting skills needs in the HR function is this: 'You know that person on your HR team that's really detail-oriented? She might want to learn another skill.' As we've seen in numerous examples, even the most detail-oriented human on the planet isn't a match for an algorithm. Machines can compute faster, work longer and make fewer errors than humans when it comes down to raw processing tasks. I know, I know. This isn't a surprise to you, but I will challenge you with this: how are you honing your own skills to prepare for a more automated workplace? More importantly, what skills should you even be focusing on?

The importance of soft skills

When we consider the applications of AI technology and the opportunities for automating an endless supply of technical tasks, the skills that will be most difficult to replicate are soft skills. Most adult professionals have taken a soft skill course here or there, and some have even had deeper dives into training and development of specific skills around leadership or other competencies. Unlike hard or technical skills, which can usually be measured by throughput or work quality, soft skills are more intangible or personality-related.

In some businesses and professions, individuals with strong technical skills can get away with a lack of soft skills. While some businesses put more value on 'how' things get done than just looking at the end result, many of them are willing to put up with highly productive performers even if they don't really get along well with others. From an HR perspective it's an incredibly common problem. But is this era of strong technical skills and poor soft skills coming to an end?

In a discussion with the CEO of one recruiting technology provider, one of his comments referenced the role of AI in levelling the playing field for workers. He believes that by focusing on what the great performers do technically that sets them apart, we can automate those types of things into the process so low-to-middle performers can increase their productivity. The question is this: when that top performer's job is automated to some degree and it levels the playing field, will businesses put up with the lack of soft skills anymore? It stands to reason that the lack of those personality characteristics will stand out much more when they aren't hidden in the shadow of top performance. This is just one more rallying cry behind the idea that soft skills will become hard requirements. Those intangible elements – including everything from teamwork and collaboration to leadership, confidence and more – will no longer be a 'nice to have' but a 'must have' for the workforce.

Still not sure? Consider the types of work that will be left over if the routine tasks are automated, whether within HR or without. Those tasks will be high-touch, very personalized and strategic to some degree. Can someone without the requisite soft skills pull that off or will they flounder? As has often been said, the soft stuff is the hard stuff. Soft skills lead to hard outcomes, and virtually any leader that has led successful teams knows this is the case.

In a related discussion with Egan Cheung, Vice President of Product at Achievers, he explained his view of how jobs will change with increasing automation. Specifically, he believes that as AI and other tools change the talent and job ecosystem, we'll see new jobs that are more focused on the things humans excel at. In other words, we're not just seeing different jobs, we're seeing more humanized jobs emerge from this trend. As a self-described technology optimist, Cheung wants to see technologies that are highly personalized to help augment the capabilities of managers in the workplace. A significant portion of employee satisfaction and engagement at work is based solely on the individual's direct manager – just think about times you worked for a really great (or really terrible) boss and you know exactly what I mean. Managers need to be guiding their people with individualized care and attention, not just a 'peanut butter spread' approach to management where all employees get the same treatment.

But to be honest, that's very challenging to pull off as a busy leader with other tasks and responsibilities, which is why it often falls off the map if it's even considered at all. Cheung says we should get to a point where systems can see what employees do well and what they need to improve, and then managers can get tailored advice and insights into how to improve employee engagement and performance. For those managers that don't have the requisite skills to manage well, algorithms can help bring them up to par. For those great managers who already do a good job of this high-touch approach, technology can help to streamline and refine their style.

If we break down jobs into their requisite tasks, the more predictable components will be more easily automated. Research from McKinsey shows that more unpredictable work, or work with a high degree of soft skills, will be harder to automate than other types of labour (Chui, Manyika and Miremadi, 2016).[9] Figure 9.1 demonstrates the range of activities in the average job. The farther down the list you go, the harder it is to automate. Replacing predictable physical activities has already happened on some assembly lines with robots, but replacing the person that manages others isn't so easy, as we observed in Chapter 7.

The rest of this chapter is dedicated to an examination of five fundamentally human skills that will become more and more important over time, regardless of the job level, function or industry. While important within HR specifically as an employee-focused function, they also have broad applicability for executives, managers and line employees across the globe. You might note that there are times that these skills overlap or complement each other in some areas, which is to be expected. If you're familiar with the story of Benjamin Franklin, one of his well-known habits was cycling through a list of 13 virtues on a regular basis to improve his faculties and performance in all areas of his life. While I can't speak to the efficacy of his own approach, that type of repetitive, intentional practice with the following list of soft skills might be the best way to start down the path to honing your own.

Those skills, in no particular order, are creativity, curiosity, compassion, collaboration and critical thinking. All of us have some of these capabilities in greater measure than others, but all of us have at least some capacity to grow and develop in each specific area. For instance,

Figure 9.1 Breakdown of average job tasks

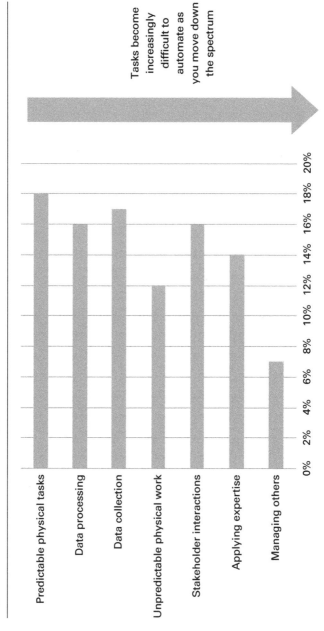

SOURCE Adapted from McKinsey & Company

creativity is one of the skills that either comes naturally for me or is spurred more readily by the types of information I consume and the white space I create for thinking. Whatever the case, it's a competency I can readily leverage at virtually any point in time. At the same time, compassion is one that I have to work harder at, because I am hard-driving and sometimes lose sight of the fact that others need my support or affirmation. That one requires more intentional effort on my part to develop. It's often been said that soft skills are easy to define and difficult to cultivate. If you walk away from this book with one overwhelming message about skills and competencies, it's my hope that you see the following list of soft skills as an opportunity to future-proof yourself against disruption from automation technologies.

Figure 9.2 Skills of the future

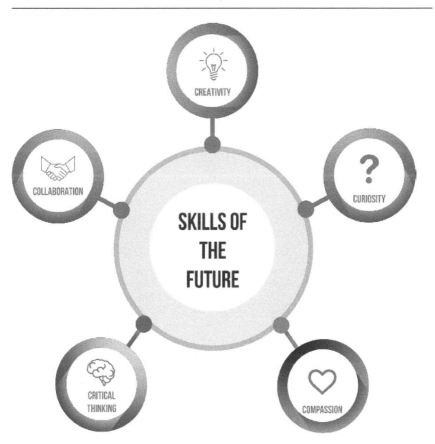

It's important to point out that the model above was designed using a mixture of interviews with business leaders and academics both inside and outside the HR function. Additionally, that research was combined with a thorough meta-analysis of a variety of research reports and data sources focusing on the future of the workforce. For example, Dr Vivienne Ming, a neuroscientist who explores the intersection of AI and child development, believes that social skills will take on increasingly important roles in a more automated world. Ming says that as jobs become more automated, even low-level roles will require more creativity and collaboration (Woodward, 2017).[10] The four categories she believes will become focal points include social skills, metacognition, creativity and personality (motivation, purpose and mindset). These points line up with a variety of other research efforts and insights from scientists, notable business leaders and industry experts. For instance, *Chief Learning Officer* magazine shared the data points shown in Figure 9.3 (Propeak, 2018)[11] to highlight soft skills that are important across a range of job roles. Regardless of whether someone holds a role as a senior executive or a line manager, these soft skills are continuing to rise in importance over time.

Figure 9.3   Future soft skill importance by role

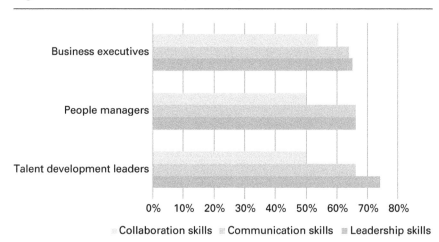

The model brings together these and other disparate sources and research efforts in academic and industry environments to paint a picture of what skills will matter most in the workplace of tomorrow.

Creativity

AlphaGo is the name of an algorithm trained to play one of the world's oldest board games – Go. Go is a strategy game that might remind you a bit of chess in that it's deceptively simple to learn but challenging to play. The object of the game is to take over sections of the board, but at the same time your opponent is attacking, countering and strategizing to outmanoeuvre you. However, unlike chess, Go has an exponentially greater number of game permutations. That's why the algorithm's creators, Google's DeepMind AI lab, focused on Go as their target game. If a computer could win at Go, then it should theoretically be able to play virtually any rules-based game. In a public exhibition with $1,000,000 in prize money on the line, AlphaGo challenged Korean world champion Go player Lee Sedol in a five-game series.

The play-by-play of this story is well chronicled online and in the documentary *AlphaGo*, but (spoiler alert) the algorithm ultimately defeated the best Go player in the world in four out of five games. Ultimately the only game won by Sedol was due to a move that commentators could only refer to as a 'brilliant move' that would 'take most opponents by surprise' (Metz, 2016).[12] When it comes to rules-based activities, whether it's a game or a business problem, algorithms have the edge. The more creativity factors into the equation, the more likely a human can outperform an AI-based technology.

Being creative is something that humans learn from a young age. Here's an experiment you can try yourself: ask any five-year-old you know to create something, and they may come back to you with an original song, a painting, or even a dance. However, it's something we 'unlearn' as we age. Ask the average 30-year-old to create something, and they will probably shrug and say they're not that creative. In truth, everyone has a creative bent in some form, but we learn to hide those things (singing in the shower, anyone?) as we age. However, in a world of increasing automation, creativity is going to be a critical edge for humans.

Consider this in a business context. When your company is trying to price a new product, having an algorithm that can examine historical pricing and predict price points is not a bad way to go. But if your business is facing new threats from competition, market constraints, or political pressures, an algorithm probably won't cut it. Rarely does an issue in the business world have clearly defined parameters and a plentiful supply of comparison data. Creativity is the solution to myriad issues, including this one.

Earlier in this chapter I mentioned Egan Cheung's take as a technology expert on how jobs will change fundamentally over time. However, one of his comments in our discussion was counter to what I would expect to hear from someone with an engineering degree and 20-plus years of putting that expertise into use as a technology leader. When I asked him about what will change from a skills perspective, he quickly replied, 'Imagination. The future is coming at us so fast, but maybe imagination is at the heart of it. The ability to dream is the source of every human advancement. Everything we've accomplished comes from someone dreaming big and then rallying groups of people around them to achieve that.' The idea that dreaming and imagination can create value is a very real concept. Need an example of why creativity matters in a business context? Individuals scoring higher on a scale of innovativeness lead businesses that see higher profits, revenues and job creation. A few years ago, researcher Dennis Stauffer set out to examine the practical impacts of innovative leaders. His research analysed entrepreneurs for their innovativeness and found that those reaching higher on the scale led businesses that were considered to be 'home runs' by investors (Stauffer, 2015).[13] Home runs were defined as those making at least a million dollars in annual revenue. Additionally, firms with more leaders scoring higher on the index saw 34 times more profits and 70 times higher revenues.

In a research study by the University of Phoenix, the educational institution found that managers overwhelmingly want their employees to be innovative and creative, yet they perceive a gap between the innovative workforce they envision and the realities of the teams they have (Workplace Innovation Survey Results, 2016).[14] Unsurprisingly, employees in the study also said they want to be creative, but they feel like their employer could do more to support the growth of creativity and the associated skills. Creativity and innovation are critical to survival in the business world, and they may be the recipe for thriving in a changing job market. Research from MIT actually shows the labour market globally shifting away from middle-skill roles towards the ends of the spectrum of high and low skills, both of which require a degree of situational adaptability (Autor, 2010).[15] That situational adaptability is essentially the ability to navigate complex situations and resolve problems on the fly, and it can happen when preparing a legal brief or delivering services as a home health aide. It comes down to being able to handle non-routine manual tasks as a key part of the job function.

Want to instil a culture of creativity in your own organization? It requires an approach that both stimulates and sustains creativity (Martins and Terblanche, 2003).[16] Employers often say they want creativity but then inadvertently take measures to standardize processes, minimize risk and diminish creative endeavours. Setting creativity into the core DNA and values of the firm and its people can help to ensure that innovation doesn't become just another thing on the 'to do' list but that it is an everyday consideration of employees, managers and executives. From a more personal perspective, improving creativity can take on a variety of flavours. Often times I've found that interdisciplinary teams and teamwork can help to create new mental connections and associations that didn't previously exist, opening up new ideas and opportunities for creative thinking. Another aspect is simply learning how to learn new things. Training isn't always learning, and learning doesn't have to include formal training, especially in a corporate context. Instead, we should explore topics and concepts that are interesting to feed our creative desires and help us to continuously expand our cognitive horizons.

From a more philosophical approach, the convenience of automation is an ever-present force that can limit our creativity. Convenience is the reward of increased automation, but struggle is one of the things that drives innovation. Automating processes to the nth degree could actually make us worse at innovating. In other words, the light bulb couldn't have been invented by continuously refining the candle – it needed an entirely different perspective. That balance of finding the right things to automate without taking too much humanity and creativity out of the process will continue to be a challenge for employers.

Innovation, creativity or imagination. Whatever you choose to call it, there is incredible value and opportunity to leverage this human trait to remain relevant and competitive both today and into the future. Is creativity something you learn? Something you are? Something you do? In reality it's a little of each of these, and we need to look for opportunities to improve creative thinking from both a personal and an organizational perspective.

Curiosity

'Why?'

If you don't have a toddler, the word 'why' might not have as much significance as it does for the parenting population. That's because the word is a way of life – a motto, even – for the preschool-age child as they explore the world around them. We are instinctively programmed to try to understand the world around us. We are inherently curious, and that gives us an edge. Why? Because algorithms do what they're told. If you run a computer program, it runs until it concludes with a finding within its parameters. However, humans are quick to ask a very simple question: 'Why?' And that simple query can drive us to find answers that may not lie on the surface or uncover questions we didn't even know we had. Humans are very well designed for handling things like nuance, poorly defined problems and ambiguity. If we don't have the answers, you'd better believe we'll find them.

John Medina, a brain researcher, spells it out plainly in his book *Brain Rules*: 'Humans are powerful and natural explorers' (Medina, 2008).[17] As Medina explains it, we are all hard-wired to be explorers in a migratory sense, but that need can be just as mental as it is physical. Curiosity is similar to creativity in that it is built into us as humans from our time as infants. Babies are always trying things to see what happens, steadily learning about the world around them over time. As we age, some of us may experiment less often because we have more 'knowns' in our lives: the stove is hot, the street is dangerous and so on. But work, especially knowledge work, requires some degree of curiosity to be successful. From a practical perspective, companies can hire someone to follow a process, or they can build an algorithm to follow a process. Over the long term, the algorithm will be cheaper to operate and less prone to mistakes. It's no different than assembly line work which has already been disrupted by robotics over the years. However, the more ambiguity and nuance that is involved, the more likely curiosity will help workers to differentiate themselves from a self-contained algorithm carrying out a predefined task.

Curiosity is more than just asking questions to learn. It's about asking questions, learning the concept and then applying it to deliver better results. From a skill-building perspective, being more curious can start with asking more questions. Consider this practical example. When I speak to executives about growing their talent analytics competencies, I encourage them to be curious. Unlike recruiting or talent management, which have pretty familiar routines and workflows, finding the right analytics to solve a problem or explore an issue is not as simple. Where will the data come from? How do we know it's connected to the problem we're trying to solve? Does it predict what we think it does, or is the result being confounded by other variables? That's where curiosity can be incredibly important, and it simply comes in the form of asking a lot of questions. Why do we measure this? How long has it been that way? Why was that decision made? What would happen if we stopped? Asking those types of open-ended questions of varying audiences will uncover different opinions, perspectives and ideas that can make us more valuable as leaders. It's not about trying to uncover an issue to pounce on – it's about trying to understand how the world works, because sometimes we don't have all the answers (even if we think we do).

Additionally, curiosity should be seen as a natural option for extending learning to improve performance. For instance, in recent years a concept called 'unschooling' has arisen which allows student interests to drive learning across various topics. The unschooling trend lets curiosity drive student learning, and it can be equally applied to adults. A personal example came a few years back when I realized I understood the general concept of calculating return on investment for a program but didn't have a firm grasp on the full model, calculation and method for gathering data and inputs and generating a thorough report of outputs and intangible benefits. I spent a dedicated block of time each week over the course of a month on researching the concept and practice, applying it in a variety of examples. Self-directed learning is an outward extension of curiosity and goes beyond the 'just Google it' mentality that each of us utilizes today when we don't know the answer to a question. Grabbing a fact from the internet isn't the same as learning an abstract concept and how to apply it. The ultimate goal of learning within the workplace context isn't just to increase knowledge – it's to increase performance. It's fitting, then, that research into types of curiosity demonstrated that being curious can improve performance (Hardy, Ness and Mecca, 2017).[18] Two varieties that exist include general and specific curiosity.

A concept that has been studied more rigorously in recent years is CQ – curiosity quotient. Unlike IQ, which is fairly static and can't be trained in workers, CQ can be to some degree. In one study researchers were able to show that intellectual curiosity actually impacts academic performance because there is some innate drive to understand concepts that may be unfamiliar. In other words, there's an insatiable 'need to know' that pushes some individuals to explore questions, unravel mysteries and solve problems (Stumm, Hell and Chamorro-Premuzic, 2011).[19] This idea that curiosity is not just something that diminishes as we age but something that is innately human and potentially a performance enabler is incredibly valuable. One leader actually used curiosity as a way to bring the best performance out of his own workforce.

In the book *Turn the Ship Around* (Portfolio, 2013), David Marquet tells the story of taking over the worst ship in the military and turning it into one of the best performers in just a few short years. He explains a wide variety of leadership concepts that led to the ultimate successful results, but one of them that sticks out is the idea of being curious instead of being questioning as a leader. His rationale for this is simple: as a leader, when you start questioning your staff they can become nervous or overwhelmed. Imagine that your own boss came to you asking why you did this or how you arrived at that solution – it could become stressful very quickly! However, when you approach the situation from a curiosity perspective, you can help to put them at ease and create a better dialogue. How much different would it feel if your own leader approached you openly to ask about how a process works or what kinds of lessons learned might be garnered from a recent project. The feeling of genuine curiosity is a truly different approach for many leaders, and as Marquet's example shows, it can lead to different results as well. Bottom line: curiosity is an incredibly important concept that lends itself to a variety of applications across the workplace and across our lives. Don't just accept that curiosity is a part of life – embrace it and encourage it in others.

Compassion

Recently my wife and I went to the movie theatre to see a film. The feature was an inspiring one, ultimately leading to a triumphant and celebratory ending. However, it was interspersed with bouts of sadness and emotion scattered throughout. I'm not normally one to get choked up by a movie, but in a few especially poignant scenes, I identified with the plight of the character on the screen. Before I knew it, I had tears brimming in my eyes. This, in essence, is compassion. Being able to understand and share the feelings of another person is a fundamentally human characteristic, whether that person is standing in front of us or on screen, as in my personal example. While few job descriptions have specifically spelled out a requirement for empathy in the past, it's one of those skills an algorithm can't easily replicate and therefore will increase in demand.

During a recent presentation at the Globoforce WorkHuman conference, Wal-Mart's Chief People Officer for Corporate Functions, Becky Schmitt, talked about the company's embrace of automation. Like virtually every retail firm, margins are low. However, for the world's biggest retailer, low prices are a permanent way of life, not a periodic sale or discount. One of the areas of focus for its automation efforts is around cashiers and the checkout process. Customers now have more options for self-checkout, allowing them to scan and bag their own groceries. Want to guess Wal-Mart's fastest-growing retail operation? Spoiler alert: it's personal shoppers. Instead of spending money on staffing those cash registers, Wal-Mart is focusing instead on hiring and/or training a bumper crop of associates who can do your grocery shopping for you. Schmitt explained that this experience has actually been even more meaningful for associates, because they are now able to interact without having to focus on a highly regimented checkout procedure. The retailer even trains its personal shoppers on how to handle a wide range of situations during the drop-off process. For example, how would you react to a young, frazzled mother with a screaming toddler in the back seat? This scenario-based training enables the associates to not only get the job done – it enables them to be compassionate and empathetic to the people they are serving. From a customer perspective, this is clearly a winning proposition.

When an algorithm diagnoses your illness, as in the example that opened this chapter, who do you ultimately want to explain that illness – a lifeless computer or an empathetic human being? The challenge for employers is in how to train workers to be more compassionate and/or empathetic. For clarity, empathy is about feeling or sharing someone's pain while compassion is more about feelings of warmth, concern, or care for another individual. An interesting piece of research shows that how the brain responds to training in each of these two areas is variable (Klimecki *et al*, 2013).[20] Participants in a study were provided with empathy training to determine how well they cope with videos depicting human suffering, and the effects were increased activity in areas of the brain that process empathy for pain. This is to be expected, right? The problem comes when someone continuously maintains a high level of empathy because they face tough situations on a regular basis, as this can lead to burnout and other negative emotions. The study was hoping to uncover ideas for how to mitigate burnout from incorporating the negative emotions of others. The next step was to determine if subsequent compassion training would reverse the negative effects associated with the video consumption, which it ultimately did. What does this mean for businesses in practical terms? Empathy is important in many roles today. Consider the Wal-Mart personal shopper example above or just look to healthcare for any number of examples where empathy would play a critical role. However, compassion training may offer a way to help workers cope with empathetic stress and improve resilience over time.

This concept of using compassion or empathy isn't just a feel-good story. There are times when hard choices have to be made, as Microsoft CEO Satya Nadella found out when he made the decision to terminate Microsoft's smartphone-focused business unit of more than 18,000 employees (Shahani, 2017).[21] In his book, *Hit Refresh* (HarperBusiness, 2017), Nadella talks about how he is pursuing a more empathetic approach to work and life, sharing some deeply personal stories and struggles that helped to shape him into the man he is today. However, even in those challenging times, compassion can guide us toward choices that need to be made; in his case, the decision to remove 18,000 employees for the sake of the 100,000-plus other workers that would be impacted if he didn't make that call. If the CEO of one of the largest companies in the world can place empathy in the top skills he wants to hone, the rest of us can make it a priority as well.

Bot versus assistant: which is better?

If I had to ask you which you would prefer, would you say bot or assistant? Some companies are taking a very careful approach to the words they use to describe these kinds of tools, because they don't want to send the wrong message to users. However, across all the technology firms I interviewed, I could not find a consistent basis for the decisions.

For example, calling an AI tool an assistant seems to be more personal, but some firms are trying to avoid the sense of AI taking over the role of an actual, human assistant. At the other end of the spectrum, some companies call their tool a bot, because it has a bit of a techie 'edge' to it. However, it can feel a little more impersonal.

At the end of the day, the use cases we've explored in this book could be satisfied by either one. However, I want you to consider it through the lens of your own team and workforce. If you're rolling out a tool or system, what term makes the most sense for how you plan to use it? Additionally, will it have a human name, or will it go by the name of its provider? As mentioned in a previous chapter, Credit Suisse uses an assistant with a human name (Amelia) to support basic IT support like password resets. Other firms use Evie, Eva, Olivia and other bots to help with meetings, and the respective bots are named by the companies that created them.

There's no definite right or wrong answer to this, but it does warrant consideration. With a heightened sense of concern around automation and job displacement, even something as simple as a name can change the perception of how people perceive the technology.

Collaboration

Consider the following scenario. You lead a team of 10 sales professionals and want to hire one more. Each of the current team members currently sells 10 units a month, or 100 total units. You might hire a superstar performer that comes in and sells 15 units, 50 per cent more than everyone else, raising your total to 115 per month. Alternatively, you might hire a great team player that sells 12 units a month but also enables the others on your team to sell 12 units each, raising the team's overall production to 132 units.

A superstar may not always improve the performance of the rest of the group. Sports is littered with examples of 'great' players hogging the spotlight and the game, ultimately leading to lower team performance. However, a great team player can dramatically improve the performance of the rest of the group. That level of collaboration is key, and it will enable workers to be increasingly valuable and competitive in the future. Collaboration is one of the skills that can be aided by AI but cannot be replaced by technology. AI can help to suggest connections or recommend mentors, but it can't connect you in a deep way with someone else. If you've ever had the strange realization that you're more connected today than ever before due to social networking tools, yet you're simultaneously more secluded than ever before from interpersonal relationships, that's exactly what I mean by this. AI can support connection and collaboration but can't replace it.

In the last HR practitioner role I held, I reported directly to the CEO. I know that CEOs can vary on a spectrum from amazing to downright awful, but mine was of high quality. He was a legitimate war hero, but if you didn't know his story you would never know that about him. He was humble but also very capable as a leader. Despite having no prior experience leading a multimillion dollar company, he worked with his co-founder to develop a flourishing business with teams in multiple countries around the globe. At the same time, this leader was amazing at building teams and influencing those around him to perform at their highest levels. Time and time again our 'small but mighty' group would compete and win against larger, better-resourced and more experienced firms.

This was backed up in research by i4cp, the Institute for Corporate Productivity. In one study by the research firm, high-performing organizations are more likely to focus on collaboration than low performers (Martin and Jamrog, 2017).[22] The data shows that those firms with the best market performance are eight times more likely to have leaders that actively help others build their networks and more than five times as likely to say that collaboration is prioritized through rewards and recognition. Employers that make collaboration and cooperation a priority see better results than those that do not. Logically we would expect this to be true, but the research shows it's more than just a buzzword.

In my own firm's research into performance management practices we found similar results. Employers with more collaborative cultures were more likely to say their approach to managing employee performance resulted in positive outcomes. That's a sharp contrast for employers with competitive or controlling cultures, who were more likely to say, paradoxically, that their approach to managing employee performance actually hampers performance and engagement. When we see our people as troublemakers that need someone to 'manage' them on a regular basis, we're going to treat people in a way that prevents them from doing their best work. On the other hand, if we look at our workers as ingredients in a recipe, we can create amazing results by finding the right combinations of individuals to solve specific kinds of problems.

Each of these components, whether cultural or managerial, factors into how employers can build a better atmosphere supportive of collaboration. But physical space is a component that impacts collaboration and interaction as well. New research into social network analysis and how organizations collaborate internally sheds additional light on this subject. In a 2018 conference presentation for the Human Capital Institute, Ben Waber, PhD, demonstrated data showing that individuals can be extremely isolated on an organizational level simply due to physical location. Even when we assume that e-mail or chat tools can overcome physical space, the data shows that employees sitting farther away from others were less likely to interact on a regular basis. His recommendation was to have workers regularly cycle through seating on a periodic basis so that each individual has a chance to build stronger networks and connections to new individuals, because physical proximity matters, even in today's digitized world. One of my favourite things to do when I worked as the HR leader for an Inc. 500-ranked fast-growing technology startup was to pack up my essential gear and move to another floor in the building once a week. I saw other employees and had important conversations with them that I might never have had if I had remained in my office on a different level, which I felt was a critical part of my performance both as an executive and as the firm's HR leader.

The Organization for Economic Co-Operation and Development (OECD) has done research around the skills that today's children need to succeed in life as they grow and mature. Their findings are fundamental, looking at components like literacy and numeracy, but one of the authors of the study also agreed that components such as 'developing passionate interests, building strong individual relationships, and participating actively in groups... will continue to be essential to create a meaningful life, no matter what happens with robots and computers'[23] (Elliott and Van Damme, 2018). Put simply: collaboration as a concept and a practice is not going to be extinct any time soon.

Think back over your career about the people you've worked with. Can you picture a handful of those that you learned from, enjoyed working with, and would work with again in a heartbeat, given the opportunity? Those are the collaborators, and they are essential for helping us as humans to perform and excel. These influential individuals motivate their peers, build deeper relationships and inspire confidence in those around them. i4cp's report also points out examples of how this plays out for a variety of employers. For instance, Patagonia is an outdoor apparel retailer renowned for its progressive culture. The company's Vice President of Human Resources, Dean Carter, says that purpose is an essential component of collaboration. It's not enough to just throw a team together with the demand that they collaborate – they need to understand the mission, vision and purpose if they are to work effectively as a group. Carter says that teams across the firm factor that into their efforts, whether solving a tricky business challenge or taking time together to serve in a volunteer capacity related to the mission of the firm.

I'll offer one final example to cement this idea that collaboration is key. Back in the mid-2000s when the United States was going through a financial downturn, the automakers were all in trouble. One of the firms, Ford, hired a new CEO in 2006 to help guide the company through the rocky times. Alan Mulally was a different kind of leader, and the firm's board hoped that his approach would be enough to help them make it back from the path they were taking. The company was losing nearly $6 billion every quarter and there was no positive end on anyone's mind (Edersheim, 2016).[24]

One of the first things Mulally instituted was a weekly business plan review meeting where senior executives shared metrics and insights into each of their areas. At the first meeting, Mulally quickly realized something was amiss. Despite the company's impending potential bankruptcy, everyone's metrics looked green, or positive. He stopped the meeting and reminded the leaders that it was their job to turn the business around, and that couldn't be done with false metrics that didn't reflect reality.

The following week, the President of Ford Americas brought a red metric into the meeting, and the rest of the executives held their breath. They were ready to watch the bloodbath begin as the new CEO took this guy apart for exposing an issue that could cost the company millions of dollars to resolve. Instead, Mulally began clapping to show his appreciation for the honesty and courage it took to bring up the problem. Then, a critical thing happened. Mulally asked the rest of the team to pitch in their ideas to help resolve the problem and get the metrics back in line. Everyone began pitching in to help, support and encourage the leader with their own advice and insights from facing similar problems in their respective areas.

By the third week, every single executive on his team brought their own red metrics, hoping to take advantage of the collaborative opportunity to work with the rest of the team in a trusting, supportive environment. Instead of competing with each other, these peers were now able to work together to solve problems that were affecting the entire business. While there were certainly other factors in Mulally's leadership approach that led to positive results for Ford, this is a critical one as it reinforced from the top down the notion of collaboration as a business imperative. The firm was able to avoid bankruptcy and turn the tide in its favour, not just surviving the downturn, but thriving in spite of it.

We can all learn from this and apply the concept back into our own workplace. Look for chances to connect people. Look for opportunities to interact with those outside your normal sphere of influence. Explore options to change your physical space or location. The quest to break down organizational silos and collaborate more effectively has been a staple of business conversations ever since, well, forever. But as the data shows, it's not just about paying lip service to the idea. True collaboration is a hallmark of a great organization in terms of both culture and performance, and each of us can start this off in our own way within our own teams and in our own professional lives.

Critical thinking

For nearly 10 years, I have worked with HR professionals who wanted to become certified. Pursuing an HR certification is one way to demonstrate competency and affirm a commitment to professional development. I have created training programmes, taught classes and offered advice to thousands of individuals seeking help with HR certification. In that time I have come to see that the number one reason people fail the HR certification exams isn't because of their experience, time spent studying, or any other common measure we might expect. In fact, it surprises me to see that the people who study most are sometimes the ones that ultimately fail. The root issue shouldn't actually surprise anyone that has actual HR experience: the students that fail do so because they can't apply the theoretical concepts they've learned to the practical questions in the exams. For example, the study text may give you an analysis of how recruitment marketing works and where it fits into the bigger talent acquisition perspective, but the question in the exam may ask you about when recruitment marketing makes sense for an employer and how the employer should invest funds for maximum impact. This lack of critical thinking is what ultimately jeopardizes the performance of the testing candidate, not a lack of knowledge. Critical thinking, as well, is a challenging skill to develop. However, it's one of those competencies that an algorithm can't easily replicate.

From the perspective of machines and humans, we'll never catch up with the amount of sheer knowledge a machine can access. When IBM's Watson beat Ken Jennings, arguably the world's best Jeopardy player, on the game show years ago, there was an interesting shift in how I personally thought about knowledge versus application. It's the difference in knowing the definition of a theory and being able to think critically about the theory's concepts to understand when to apply it to a situation. The balance of theory versus practical application and execution is a very common problem for one population: college graduates. Someone exiting college believes they know what they need to know in order to get and succeed in a job, right? Actually, Gallup's research shows an alarming gap between what educators think about how well they prepare for the workforce and what business leaders think about how much education prepares people for the workforce (Busteed, 2014).[25] According to the study, 96 per cent of Chief Academic Officers rate their educational institution as effective at preparing students for the realities of the working world. That sounds positive until you attempt to reconcile it with the views of the businesses that hire those former students: just one in ten business leaders believe that graduates have the skills and competencies their businesses need to remain competitive.

This is due in part to that gap in critical thinking. There's not an employer in the world that would ask its candidates to forgo critical thinking or that would deprioritize that concept in the hiring process, yet businesses so often substitute educational achievement (degree, GPA and so on) in place of any evidence of critical thought. Even experience on the job doesn't necessarily prove someone's critical thinking capabilities. The concept from the creativity component earlier in this chapter of 'learning how to learn' is critical here. We have been conditioned to expect the answer to a question and have, in some instances, lost the ability or the initiative to creatively think through the problem and solve it. By helping to build that skill of analysing a problem, understanding the cause and developing potential solutions, we can help to teach critical thinking as a hard concept for business leaders. As mentioned in Chapter 8, one of the challenges of using AI is a lack of context. Even if there is plentiful data, machines are designed to move from point A to point B. Machines do not ask if point B is even the right destination.

In the last few years I've run a wide assortment of workshops that are essentially HR hackathons. In these sessions, I coach business leaders on how to frame an issue they are facing, break it down into its smaller pieces and then solve a small piece of the puzzle. We have plenty of resources helping us with our five-year plans or our annual strategies, but there are some problems that need a small, immediate solution. For example, one firm last year was facing issues with its candidate experience due to some members of the recruiting team not following the established procedures and best practices. Within 20 minutes we had come up with a handful of ways to resolve the issue, from using the 'best' recruiters as change agents and champions to using a leaderboard to highlight the spectrum of candidate experience scores by name, putting some positive peer pressure on the recruiters to improve their results. The way you know you've arrived at a good solution in this exercise is that you nearly smack yourself for not thinking of the relatively simple idea sooner. These kinds of hackathons can help us to practise the critical thinking and reasoning skills we need to thrive as business leaders.

MIT research points out that leaders who can create very focused problem statements, a process of defining an issue or challenge in detail, are actually more productive and perform better than their peers with less focus (Kinni, 2017).[26] Isn't that interesting? Those individuals who can define problems best are more likely to perform better than those that can't. When you think about it from a practical standpoint, it makes sense that defining an issue correctly means you can get right to work on solving it. But how often do employers treat the symptoms of a problem for years without actually attacking the root cause?

This discussion about soft skills is wrapped up perfectly by a quote from one of Deloitte's senior Canadian leaders, Gordon Sandford: 'If you train yourself to be a robot, then you're out of a job' (The Intelligence Revolution, nd).[27] For now we're not fighting, literally or figuratively, against robots for most knowledge worker jobs. But there may come a time when more of the work that we're doing is going to be overcome and automated by the various tools and technologies that are being developed in laboratories around the world. That said, Sandford's sentiment is one to keep in mind: differentiate your skills or face the consequences. We have control over our own capabilities. Instead of feeling helpless or powerless against a tide of oncoming technological change, we can brace ourselves by honing those core human competencies that separate us from robots and algorithms. Whatever happens with the advances in AI technology, you're in control of your own development, growth and capabilities.

A final question

In all of this discussion about people and the technology that supports them, I have debated with myself relentlessly on a very important question. *Does technology make work more human or less human?* To be honest, I think it's pretty clear that I'm a technological optimist. I believe in the power and value that technology can bring. We have the power to make work more human, not less, with the advent of AI technologies and tools. Work can finally be more human than ever. Ironically, one of the most feared advances in technology, the development and adoption of AI, is what it ultimately took to get us to this precipice. This fundamental human act of working, whether as an employee, a contractor, or some other type of resource, is truly enabled by AI technologies.

Because of the systems we have explored in the pages of this book, work can be greatly more human. The 'black hole' of resumes where candidates apply and never hear a response? Today those candidates can connect with helpful chatbots that offer them a conversation, an opportunity to express their interests and a chance to ask burning questions. And people actually thank the bots for those discussions! Learning technologies can help us to teach people in individualized ways that help them learn best – no more cramming everyone into a classroom for every single training need. And finally, we can manage to the individual using engagement and talent management tools that give us a full view of someone's true capabilities and interests.

If nothing else, at least consider the skills component we discussed in this chapter. By honing your own critical soft skills, you can prepare yourself and your workforce for a more automated future. The advance of technology is inevitable, but your skills and capabilities don't have to become outdated, outmoded, or obsolete. Focus on growing your compassion so you can meet the needs of the human workforce you interact with. Build up your curiosity by asking questions, exploring unexplored concepts and connecting with new people and ideas. Expand your collaboration by meeting with other leaders around the world using virtual tools and platforms while simultaneously deepening your connections with those people closest to you in the workplace. Don't ever feel like you're powerless in the face of technological change, even something as powerful and far-reaching as AI, because you are ultimately capable of managing your own destiny.

Key points

- As automation occurs, the work that remains will become increasingly 'human' in nature. Therefore, developing and refining those core human skills will be necessary to long-term stability.

- Five key areas of skills exist that help to set us apart from what machines can accomplish: creativity, curiosity, compassion, collaboration and critical thinking.

- Above all else, technology enables work to become more human. And as business leaders, HR executives and those who care about the workforce, this is a very positive outcome.

Notes

1 https://www.livescience.com/55145-ai-boosts-cancer-screen-accuracy.html

2 https://www.cnbc.com/2018/05/15/technology-careers-top-traits-for-success-from-paypal.html

3 https://www.wired.com/story/watch-boston-dynamics-spotmini-robot-open-a-door/

4 https://www.theguardian.com/world/2015/jul/16/japans-robot-hotel-a-dinosaur-at-reception-a-machine-for-room-service

5 https://www.weforum.org/agenda/2017/02/nearly-half-of-jobs-could-be-automated-in-the-future-heres-what-the-researchers-are-saying

6 https://www.sdworx.be/en/sd-worx-r-d/publications/press-releases/2017-12-12-european-hr-professionals-see-the-emergence-of-artificial-intelligence-as-a-threat

7 http://www.pewinternet.org/2014/08/06/future-of-jobs/

8 https://www.theguardian.com/science/alexs-adventures-in-numberland/2015/mar/13/pi-day-2015-memory-memorisation-world-record-japanese-akira-haraguchi

9 https://www.mckinsey.com/business-functions/digital-mckinsey/our-insights/where-machines-could-replace-humans-and-where-they-cant-yet

10 https://www.thriveglobal.com/stories/11908-preparing-our-kids-for-an-ai-world-neuroscientist-on-why-social-skills-matter-more-than-ever

11 http://www.clomedia.com/2018/05/07/digital-future-human/

12 https://www.wired.com/2016/03/go-grandmaster-lee-sedol-grabs-consolation-win-googles-ai/

13 https://www.emeraldinsight.com/doi/full/10.1108/IJIS-03-2016-001

14 http://www.phoenix.edu/about_us/media-center/news/workplace-innovation-survey-results.html

15 https://economics.mit.edu/files/5554

16 https://www.emeraldinsight.com/doi/full/10.1108/14601060310456337

17 Medina, J (2008) *Brain Rules: 12 principles for surviving and thriving at work, home, and school,* Pear Press, Seattle, WA

18 http://psycnet.apa.org/record/2016-48348-040

19 http://www.hungrymindlab.com/wp-content/uploads/2015/10/von-Stumm-et-al-2011.pdf

20 https://www.ncbi.nlm.nih.gov/pubmed/22661409

21 https://www.npr.org/sections/alltechconsidered/207/09/25/553431516/how-do-you-turn-around-a-tech-giant-with-empathy-microsoft-ceo-says

22 https://s3.amazonaws.com/assets.i4cp.com/files/0020/2836/Purposeful_Collaboration-i4cp-2017.pdf?AWSAccessKeyId=AKIAJAKOI6IRMPGICZXA&Expires=1524240067&Signature=gqi16qqUM69JhrFhN9UXIdtPvJE%3D

23 https://medium.com/edmodoblog/the-global-search-for-education-are-you-as-good-as-your-robot-9a14d117eeb8

24 https://www.brookings.edu/blog/education-plus-development/2016/06/28/alan-mulally-ford-and-the-6cs/

25 http://news.gallup.com/opinion/gallup/173249/higher-education-work-preparation-paradox.aspx

26 https://www.inc.com/theodore-kinni/theres-one-question-you-must-ask-before-solving-any-problem-its-also-the-most-un.html

27 https://www2.deloitte.com/content/dam/Deloitte/ca/Documents/human-capital/ca-EN-HC-The-Intelligence-Revolution-FINAL-AODA.pdf

AFTERWORD

Since I sat down the very first time to start writing this book, the variety and depth of AI technologies in the marketplace has already changed dramatically. It's strange, really, because I feel as if I'm shooting at a moving target. If I was writing about gravity or some other universal constant, the research and practice around the topic would have remained fairly static throughout the writing process. However, when you're looking at a new field with cutting-edge developments occurring virtually every day, it's a bit different.

The reason I wrote this book was due in part to the need for an unbiased viewpoint on this concept. So much of the information I see on a daily basis around this topic is either wildly overhyped, too theoretical or technical for the average practitioner to understand and apply, or downright incorrect. As an independent researcher I have the freedom to explore the topic to my heart's content and talk about the good, the bad and the ugly. However, a company developing these technologies has a vested interest in telling the positive side of the story, often elevating it to the level of marketing hype. Additionally, my focus on the practical impacts keeps me from being too academic in my approach, which is a good thing for the millions of employees at companies I have supported over the years. They need more than theory to get the job done, to get the product shipped and to manage a highly complex workforce – they need actionable intelligence.

As the range of solutions that leverage machine learning and AI technologies become more prevalent and integrated into the human capital industry, my hope is that these issues of hype and theory dwindle away or are at least replaced by relevant and practical information that supports those that need it most. Why? Because we *need* technologies like this.

It's pretty clear where I stand on the matter. Technology has the power to radically improve the experience for candidates, employees and the rest of the company if used properly. However, is it smart to expect that every employer is going to approach this with the right frame of mind?

As I neared the completion of the book, I saw several news items come out criticizing the use of AI because of concerns about bias or a fear of causing the hiring process to become dehumanized. I have addressed these items within the context of the book from the perspective of an HR or business leader, but for candidates and the public at large it can absolutely seem to be very exclusionary to be shunted off to an algorithm instead of having the chance to interact with a real person. It leads me to believe that there is a need for ethical standards to help guide vendors as they develop the technology and for business leaders as they seek to implement systems that include AI components. After all, with great power comes great responsibility. I have been open about my optimism here, and what I feel compelled to point out is that technology advances have always been and will continue to be a fact of life. From the first light bulb to the smartphone, technology is always evolving. The unchanging component is the people behind the technology.

The truth is that we, as people, have the capability to dehumanize virtually anything, and that includes processes that have technology involved or not. People are ultimately the ones that decide how to treat others, whether they use a piece of technology or do it in person. At the same time, we have the opportunity to create incredibly positive experiences for people. Some companies around the world are known for their ability to create amazing customer experiences that drive brand loyalty and value for the business. Those firms are able to create raving fans for their products and services by treating everyone with respect and appreciation. We need to approach the people side of the business with the very same perspective. Let's use the things that AI can do to scale up and deliver incredibly human experiences that leave candidates and employees feeling like they received white glove service, even if it's being ultimately delivered by a computer.

I have come to the realization after years of researching and writing about technology that it's usually not about the technology at all. Funny enough, it really is all about people. I hope you walk away with the knowledge that in spite of the technological advances and changes, the revolutionary capabilities, and the continued development and exploration of AI systems, it still comes back to people. That's ultimately why I decided to finish the book with a discussion around the fundamental human skills that we can't let lapse or diminish in importance. If we have those critical skills around compassion, creativity and so on then we can ensure that we're always on the right path with our technology decisions. If we *only* make decisions based on profit margins, we'll make choices that take us down an unhealthy path.

One of the recent research projects I had an opportunity to participate in required me to envision what AI will look like in the next 10 years. It was an interesting activity that gave me a chance to stretch my thinking, but ultimately like all of those predictions about jobs and robots it was no more than an educated guess. What I do know is that today, there are some great opportunities to leverage technology, and some of those technologies have AI within them, extending their capabilities beyond what we've seen historically. Every facet of our personal lives is being impacted by these ever-evolving systems and tools, including economically and socially. Work is such a big part of life for the people that companies employ, and if there's an opportunity to use technology to make that work experience more human to some degree, we should absolutely take it.

Thanks for reading this book and for your own commitment to learning about the opportunities these technologies bring. Above all, stay human, my friends.

INDEX